Is He Ever Going to Leave His Wife?

The Answers to the Questions You Desperately Want to Know

MARTESS A DOWLING

First published by Ultimate World Publishing 2023
Copyright © 2023 Martess Dowling

ISBN

Paperback: 978-1-922828-97-2
Ebook: 978-1-922828-98-9

Martess Dowling has asserted her rights under the Copyright, Designs and Patents Act 1988 to be identified as the author of this work. The information in this book is based on the author's experiences and opinions. The publisher specifically disclaims responsibility for any adverse consequences which may result from use of the information contained herein. Permission to use information has been sought by the author. Any breaches will be rectified in further editions of the book.

All rights reserved. No part of this publication may be reproduced, stored in or introduced into a retrieval system, or transmitted in any form, or by any means (electronic, mechanical, photocopying, recording or otherwise) without the prior written permission of the author. Any person who does any unauthorised act in relation to this publication may be liable to criminal prosecution and civil claims for damages. Enquiries should be made through the publisher.

Cover design: Ultimate World Publishing
Layout and typesetting: Ultimate World Publishing
Editor: Carmela Julian Valencia
Cover Image Copyrights:
Sandra van der Steen-Shutterstock.com
zimmytws-Shutterstock.com

Ultimate World Publishing
Diamond Creek,
Victoria Australia 3089
www.writeabook.com.au

Dedication

This book is dedicated to Janet Marie Norton, beautiful friend called back to heaven.

Testimonials

Really good premise and love the playful attitude that you take in writing; makes it less heavy, which is helpful. All said with love and curiosity.

Jeremy and Tim

It is easy reading but gets the point across very well. I can see many women thinking to themselves, 'This is my story and that's exactly what he said to me.'

Trudy Green

They were easy to read, with a little bit of gentle wry humour, yet still with the points you want to get across still coming through.

Josie Evans

Very well written as well as it grabs the reader's attention and leaves the reader wanting more. A real page turner.

Sharon Budge

Contents

Dedication	iii
Testimonials	v
Preface	1
Introduction: You Have Picked Up This Book Because You Are at a Crossroads…	5
Chapter 1: In the Beginning …	9
Chapter 2: You're What? Married?	13
Chapter 3: Women Love Bad Boys	17
Chapter 4: Is All This Stemming From Your Childhood?	21
Chapter 5: OK, So Where Do You Go From Here?	25
Chapter 6: The Fallout	29
Chapter 7: OK, It's Truth Time	33
Chapter 8: Throw Down the Gauntlet	39
Chapter 9: Moving on Today	45
Chapter 10: You Can Try and Change His Mind	51
Chapter 11: What If You Already Know He Is Married?	57
Chapter 12: The Polyamory Relationship	61
Chapter 13: Why Men Cheat	65
Chapter 14: All Narcissists Are Not Created Equal	71
Chapter 15: Narcissistic Behaviour and How It Affects You	77
Chapter 16: The Wife's Perspective and When 'It Hits the Fan'	85

Chapter 17: Where Did It All Go Wrong for Him?	91
Chapter 18: An Affair Can Be the Best Thing for a Marriage	95
Chapter 19: What About the Kids?	99
Chapter 20: How Long Is This Going to Take?	105
Chapter 21: He Is Not Afraid to Lose You	109
Chapter 22: Dumped by a Married Man	115
Chapter 23: How to Stop Being Obsessed With a Married Man	121
Chapter 24: What Not to Do	127
Chapter 25: Going Through the Grief	133
Chapter 26: How to Heal From This	139
Chapter 27: What If He Wants to Come Back?	143
Chapter 28: The Stigma of Being the Other Woman	147
Chapter 29: Why Am I Always Attracting Married Men?	153
Chapter 30: The Office Romance Gone Bad	157
Chapter 31: His Loss	161
Chapter 32: A Word About Your Inner Voice	165
Chapter 33: Recovery Road	169
Chapter 34: Take Back Your Power, Girl!	175
Chapter 35: To Sum Up His Excuses	181
Chapter 36: He **Will** Leave His Wife if …	185
Chapter 37: Breakdown as to Why He Is **NOT** Leaving His Wife	191
To Sum Up	199
Endnotes	201
Acknowledgements	203
About the Author	205

Preface

This book was written by a woman for women. However, the subject matter can apply equally to anyone involved with someone in another permanent and committed relationship.

I had worked in various jobs – one of them being a reader on a tarot line. And the most frequent question asked was, 'Is he ever going to leave his wife?' After countless conversations of this nature, I then began to do some research from many different sources. The more I talked with these women, I began to realise two things:

First, this situation was all too common; a couple seeing each other in secret, living mostly in the shadows, stealing moments of intimacy where they could, and leaving you, the Other Woman, in a constant state of yearning while the married man went back to his wife.

Second, these Other Women had few recourses to support and guide them unless they sought the help of a professional counsellor. I also found they mostly could not share their affair with anyone. They stayed alone, waited and hoped things would change and they would one day be together.

The idea for this book came about after numerous conversations with these Other Women, each with a heart-wrenching story about their experience with their married man – which sometimes lasted for years. They needed sound advice and practical solutions and wanted some way of answering the burning questions they all shared about dating their married man, hence the call to the tarot line.

The fact their situation is still as relevant today as ever remains irresistible. People from all walks of life, backgrounds, religions, economic status or position conducted extramarital affairs – sometimes to their own detriment. Despite the consequences, the magnetism for such a life choice never dissuaded them from seeking happiness elsewhere. This prompted me to research the *why* factor. The more I understood, the more I wanted to share what I had learned. Eventually, I wrote this book in the hope that you begin to understand the dynamics at play and do what is needed to take control of your life and shape your future.

So, if you are in such a relationship and need direction or answers, this book is for you. I ask you to keep an open mind and act on your gut feelings. By the end, you will be in a much clearer, calmer and more empowered position to make sound choices and take responsibility for your betterment in the life and happiness you seek.

I will be straight and honest with you. I am not here to judge or hurt you but to help you understand you do have choices. Some things in this book will be hard to read, and I am sorry

Preface

for that. But the truth will set you free, and I'll give you practical ways to achieve that level of happiness and security you deserve. So, let's do this!

INTRODUCTION

You Have Picked Up This Book Because You Are at a Crossroads…

You love this man deeply and want with all your heart to be with him permanently, but there is one major hitch … he is already married!

You, no doubt, have questions. You may be confused and even frustrated at the whole situation with this man, and there will be one question burning within you: Is he ever going to leave his wife?

This book is all about you and about understanding the emotions you are experiencing. From the many conversations I have had with women like you, they all came to a point where they could no longer continue as they had been and needed to make some tough calls. A reset was needed with a new way of thinking where they could empower themselves. They would no longer operate from a position of helplessness or be too frightened of missing an opportunity with their man and losing him prematurely if they rocked the boat. The what-if questions became irrelevant.

To begin with, they were clearly not equipped and certainly not strong enough to make any life-changing decisions. This is where Is He Ever Going to Leave His Wife? can help you. With the step-by-step chapters of information and scenarios, you will be guided to make informed and sound choices for yourself. Because it is **All About You!**

Empowering yourself to trust your feelings, making yourself a priority, having **your** well-being considered first and foremost and bringing **your** happiness to the top of the list are vital in building your inner and mental strength. What you are looking for now is that break in the clouds, some peace, clarity and your sanity restored. But most of all, you begin to understand your right to happiness, which is the foundation for building a great future. Your future!

Much of what I have written were first-hand accounts of women who were navigating an affair. I discovered that all affairs are not born equal and that affairs have changed with the advent of technology.

Now more than ever, affairs are easier to achieve – whether in real life or virtual. So many more people are getting involved in extramarital activities as a diversion to cope with the stresses of life, for excitement with someone different, to break from

You Have Picked Up This Book Because You Are at a Crossroads...

reality and escape into their private world or for a myriad of personal reasons.

We will explore how and why this affair started and why you fell in love with each other. Although it sounds simple enough, an affair is never as straightforward as people think. The dynamics are completely different from that of a married man to that of a single man. There are no set formulae as to how things will turn out with your affair because every situation is different and every person within the relationship brings a unique perspective to overcome. But there are ways in which you can look after yourself and lessen the emotional ups and downs through knowledge, understanding and regaining your power.

We will also take a fresh look at why you are hooked on this relationship and why it is important to consider yourself first. Let there be no mistake here – an affair is all about him and his needs. Instead of always relinquishing your power to keep him happy, because maybe someday he will be with you, let's work on realistic ways to change the dynamics of this relationship to give both of you what you really want.

Why he has not left his wife is the most pressing issue you are trying to comprehend, and rightly so. Therefore, we will look at the reasoning as to why actions speak louder than words and what you can do to help him if he is having trouble leaving his marriage.

You need practical ways to start putting yourself first, treating yourself as a priority, taking responsibility for your happiness, gaining confidence and making the best version of yourself. It's a win-win situation, no matter how you look at it.

Is He Ever Going to Leave His Wife?

So, treat this book like a road map you can reference and understand what is happening within your relationship, make sound decisions about what you will and won't put up with and actively change your situation.

CHAPTER 1

In the Beginning …

So, this is your world – being with a man who is everything you dreamed. The excitement and thrill of seeing him, being with him and spending those precious moments with him light you up; nothing comes close. You live for the time to be with him, and the more you see him, the more you want him as a permanent in your life.

Your world is complete. **You** are the most beautiful, passionate, enchanting, intelligent woman he has ever met, and he can't get enough of you. While **he** is the most gorgeous man that God ever put breath in, and everything about him completes you.

You have met the man of your dreams, and your happiness scale is somewhere beyond the stratosphere. He loves you – you know he loves you by his actions – so there is no doubt you were destined to be together. Life is great.

Is He Ever Going to Leave His Wife?

You continue seeing each other, and all your hopes and dreams have come true. He is attentive, considerate, generous, warm, funny, so intelligent and a man you can be proud of – and you can't wait to show him off to all your friends and family! With all this wonderfulness in your life – all because of this beautiful man – you know whoever meets him is going to be so happy for you, and they are going to just love him. No doubt they will ask, 'So, when's the wedding?'

It is like being on a permanent honeymoon, and all that needs to happen is for him to take the next step and maybe move in together. It would be perfect – he doesn't have to drive all the way across the city to see you, and you can do so much more together because you will be with each other.

Time passes, and a feeling you just can't shift begins to creep in.

'But life is wonderful …' you say to yourself. 'He is wonderful. We are so happy together, and everything is just great, and there is no wedding ring on his finger …'

But that niggling feeling persists, and you start to think, *Am I missing something? Is this all too good to be true?*

That is when you take a closer look at those 'little' things that seem out of sync with him. You know little about him other than what he told you, and most of that was about his work or when he was growing up. So, why is this gorgeous man still single? 'Maybe he is too good to be true!'

Whether he tells you himself, or you eventually find out another way – perhaps you unexpectedly see him with another woman too old to be his daughter and too young to be his mother,

In the Beginning ...

and you know he doesn't have a sister, cousin, or niece; or maybe you spot him having coffee with another woman (Yes, but that could be a work colleague); or, unthinkably, someone tells you he has a wife (Wife? What wife?); or perhaps in time you simply trusted your gut and figured it out yourself – HE'S MARRIED!

This heart-shattering news about the secret he has kept from you, however it is delivered, has your life taking a screeching halt, and this revelation just blew your world out of the water. The feelings surging within have rocked you to the core, and this monumental struggle is going on in your head as to what to do now. Within the span of moments, you go through the entire seven stages of grief and become conflicted about how you will deal with this. You are stunned motionless!

But wait, there's more! When you confront him, he tells you he doesn't love his wife, that he is with her because (fill in the blank), and he wants out of his marriage. But he loves you and wants to be with you, make a future with you. He is just getting things sorted before he starts divorce proceedings. It wasn't worth saying anything because the ball is already rolling in that department, so why worry you? (What a considerate man – all that concern about your mental health and feelings! What a guy!)

OK, your mind implodes, and your feelings for him hit the emotional brakes as you briefly come to your senses, which at this point is a good thing because thoughts of you making headlines in the morning's paper appear as you catch yourself reaching for the nearest heavy object to smack and end him with.

Is He Ever Going to Leave His Wife?

He is undoubtedly looking pitiful, all misery and despair in that gorgeous exterior, so you do exactly what any woman would do – you comfort him! Now he's hooked you!

If, however, you have the iron will of Margaret Thatcher, then you let go of the heavy object you are about to hurl and tell him to leave – right after he tries to cajole you into overlooking this slight inconvenience of him being married.

Now you are at a crossroads!

---

*Take inspiration from the song
'Ironic' by Alanis Morisette.*

CHAPTER 2

You're What? Married?

After the bombshell hit of this trivial, barely significant fact he has just admitted to, the tempo for this dance ramps up a notch. Of course, he's made sure to tell you (again) how unhappy he is with his wife, who, incidentally, is the biggest (insert appropriate names he's called her) in heels who has ever walked the face of this earth.

He is very convincing, and because you love him, you believe what he says. Why wouldn't you? Up until the news broke about him being married, you trusted him with your life and, on that point, from your position, he's hoping nothing has changed.

But the dynamics of your relationship have instantly transformed because now he is looking to you as an ally, a friend he can count on, the salve to his wounds and the safe place he can come to when his married life gets overwhelming. How special are you? Besides, you are the one he 'really' loves because only you understand him. So, your position from this moment on is not only to provide him with intimacy, counselling and a haven to retreat to, but now your role is that of a mistress.

At this moment, your brain engages from the shock, and you ask, 'But why don't you just leave her if things are that bad?'

OK, brace yourself. This is where he tells you, 'I can't leave because of the kids!'

HE'S GOT KIDS? That's another 'little' fact he conveniently omitted to mention, and this is where your mind preps itself for a meltdown. KIDS?

So, he begins to explain about 'the kids', and your sharp Spidey senses start to bristle. Within no time, your brain starts coding and firing answers to his excuses at the rate of an M15. But instead of voicing your feedback on what he is saying, everything remains locked in your head. For some reason, you have lost the ability to speak.

He might say something like, 'They are still young.' (Young? How young? How long have you guys been together?)

Or 'They need a stable home life.' (Their father is having an affair. How stable can their home life be if you meet with me four nights a week?)

Then there is, 'This is their final year of high school.' (So, they are young adults who have an attitude and spend as little time with their parents as possible!)

You're What? Married?

But the real clanger is when he says, 'I just can't leave my kids.' (OK. Really? But you are happy to leave them in the care of the psycho you call your wife four nights a week. Yeah, I can see your reasoning!)

All the while, you are just staring at him, saying nothing. It is a little-known fact that women are at their most dangerous when they either say nothing to a man or speak quietly in short sentences, fixing him with a laser-beam stare.

If the kids were not a major hurdle for him to leave, two other significant conditions might present where he can't leave because of his 'wife'.

First, she may be ill, and he is decent enough not to abandon her at this time. Depending on the illness, it is not appropriate that he forsakes her, and it is unthinkable that he treats her with such disregard while she is ill. (Amber warning alert!)

If his wife is terminal, then he needs to be with her. She may want him to carry on with his life and may even want him to find someone else to look after him, but he also needs to be physically present with her to support and comfort her in the time she has left. There is no place for another party to enter the equation during this phase. Support and encourage him to do the right thing by her and assure him of your understanding over his situation. Despite this being hard on you both, he must do right by his wife. He will respect you for your understanding and himself for being the better man.

Second, suppose he is tangled up with his wife like an overgrown bramble and shares a sizeable portfolio, assets or is in business with her (Is all the money in her name? Well, of

Is He Ever Going to Leave His Wife?

course, it is!). In that case, this will be much trickier for him to extricate himself from the marriage, especially because of the ramifications to the business, and their divorce lawyers will then happily take a chunk of anything they both own.

Yes, there might also be a host of reasons he may give you why he has not left the marriage – some will be more legitimate than others. But from your standpoint, understand that, on the whole, these are nothing more than **excuses**, not 'valid' reasons for him to stay with his wife. You need to understand the difference.

OK, what now? The best course at this moment is to politely ask him to leave (Yes, I am serious!), as you need time apart to think about what has just come to light and reflect on what he has told you. Without a doubt, you will meet with resistance here because he does not want you to alter things; after all, he is quite happy keeping the status quo. But you need some alone time to calm down, take in what has happened and what he has just admitted to, put aside your feelings for him and give this matter serious consideration once he has left.

Before he goes, ask him to leave you alone until you contact him. This is your chance to breathe, give yourself some room to think and evaluate your situation without his influence. You cannot rationally think when he is still there. Well, you never could think straight whenever he was in your vicinity, but that was for an entirely different reason!

CHAPTER 3

Women Love Bad Boys

Perhaps, during his absence, you are thinking how much you love all the attention, how he makes you feel, and you can't get enough of him. He is exciting, somewhat dashing and daring, and there is this irresistible magnetism and element of danger about him. He is a man's man, and his commanding presence and air of power are heady stuff. You have fallen in love with a bad boy.

If you are honest with yourself, there is no chance on this side of heaven that you'd want to let him go. He makes you feel alive, and your life is so thrilling. The idea that you are his secret, passion and desire is what fuels your love for him.

Who wouldn't want to be adored and treated like a goddess by such a man? Every time you are together is like nothing you have ever experienced. Secret phone calls and texts are risky enough to give you both that forbidden pleasure because there will always be the chance of him getting caught. The fact that he loves the chase, element of danger and getting away with this illicit affair with you is as intoxicating for him as it is for you.

You would anticipate his arrival, and you are either whisked off to dinner somewhere special. Perhaps after, you share a room at an exclusive hotel where you both live out your fantasy in sumptuous surroundings. Or maybe you have the perfect seduction in play at your place. You have cleaned, changed to fresh sheets, cooked a fabulous meal and are wearing something he loves that shows off your figure to perfection.

It is one of the most wonderful feelings to be loved and appreciated in this way. In a sense, being with a married man allows you to fall in love with each other repeatedly because you are only seeing each other a few times a week (if not less), so the anticipation of your rendezvous contributes to this factor.

With dating a single man, where the intoxication of love happens at the beginning and eases into a mutual and loving relationship, you have the time and frequency to get to know him – the real him. The first rush of love gently settles, and if this man is the real deal for you, then your experience is one of a soul connection with each other. The married man, however, is a power-packed adrenalin rush. If the relationship remains on this casual but intense course, it is nothing but utter bliss – stealing moments together, mind-blowing sex and a love that can only be described as euphorically unreal! Because that is exactly what it is – unreal!

As time goes by, however, the relationship with your married man begins to settle – just like the single couple who have been dating for a time, going from the first phase of the relationship (crazy sex) to real love and companionship. With your married man, however, you get stuck in the first phase for much longer because you do not see each other as often as you would both like; the relationship's illicit nature keeps it in fantasy mode.

When normalcy creeps in, however, you find how unreal your relationship has been. You see the real side of your married man because he has 'normalcy' everyday with his wife and family. Now that your relationship with him is progressing in that direction, one of two things will happen. Ever heard the expression 'Familiarity breeds contempt'?

Once that conversation happens about him leaving his wife, because 'you are so great together' and you love him deeply, he will either postpone the 'leaving' bit for as long as he can, to which you will always be waiting for him and 'that' will grind you down. Or, he may decide that while you are fun to play with, the thrill he craves is no longer as intense. So, he dumps you and moves onto someone fresh, and it's like having a bucket of cold water thrown over you if this happens.

Heartbreak like that is indescribable, but trying to sustain that euphoric relationship is unrealistic because you are dealing with a rush junkie, a serial cheater and a user – a bad boy! Therefore, it is important to look after your heart, your self and your well-being. While you have no contact with this man, you can decide whether your heart is prepared for the kind of pain only a lover can give you.

CHAPTER 4

Is All This Stemming From Your Childhood?

OK, bear with me here. This may be a delicate but vital chapter for you to read, and it is written with the utmost respect towards you.

Let's look at a personal snapshot of your past – when you were a kid – and what life was like growing up for you with your family or carers. This is where you will find the answers to your current conflicts.

What patterns we develop as children follow us to adulthood, so maybe the possible reason you are even involved with a married man could stem from those early years within the family dynamic. Look back at how your parents or primary caregivers interacted with each other and their family members.

Is He Ever Going to Leave His Wife?

Were there a happy home and people who supported and cared about each other and showed respect and love to their children? Was your home a harmonious and nurturing environment to live in, where conflict could be resolved peacefully and without anger, shame or threats?

Chances are, if you lived in a positive and nurturing environment, you grew up with a strong and constructive sense of self, your mental health developed in a positive and wholesome way, and you were supported with a firm belief in your worth. Your parents treated you as an integral part of the family, and your opinions and ideas were respected and encouraged. They placed value on you as a person, and you made a difference.

Those who were fortunate enough to have been nurtured in a positive home environment developed a healthy attitude towards themselves and any relationships in their adult lives. How they perceived their role in that family stems from how they were treated and will reflect their experiences. Although, individually, the case for nature versus nurture will also have a significant bearing.

Sadly, not everyone grew up with such positive influences. Their home life was not a place of nurturing, or such dysfunctional elements within the family dynamics impacted them negatively in some way.

Perhaps you were not given the framework for love and support you needed, thus enforcing the belief that acceptance from your parent or caregivers was unattainable. So, in your adult life, you subconsciously formed a relationship with an unattainable man.

Is All This Stemming From Your Childhood?

Our main caregivers did the best they could with the abilities they had, but they were not equipped to deal with the complexities of family life. Their level of growth, again, depended on how they were brought up and treated. So, unless there was an opportunity to evolve through awareness and personal understanding, the pattern of dysfunction would continue.

Simply put, we are the product, in many respects, of our upbringing. We look to what is familiar and recognisable in our relationships because that is what we relate to and understand (Ever heard the term 'You married someone exactly like your parent'?). So, this married man is not only reinforcing your beliefs about what you have accepted to be true about yourself but also giving you what you think you deserve.

If you reach into your core and look at why you are settling for the crumbs this married man is giving you, it might not be surprising to find you are still trying to correct the patterns (or damage) of the past. You could still be trying to gain acceptance from a parental dynamic that did not provide the balanced love you needed, which has carried through to your intimate connections.

Look at the relationship with that parent (or both parents) and how they shaped you, instilled beliefs about yourself and influenced you to make the decisions you have. This may go a long way to explaining behaviours regarding how you subconsciously may still be trying to gain their acceptance, relinquishing responsibility and what you are doing with this married man.

It is easy to blame your parents for the shortcomings you face, and while they gave you those foundations, it does not mean you are stuck with the cards you were dealt. On the contrary, you are now a grown woman who can make decisions for yourself, and if you can recognise the patterns of the past, then you can break them.

Seeking help from a professional psychologist or counsellor is the best thing you can do to change those past patterns. Read books about personal growth or childhood traumas. An excellent book titled How to Overcome Your Childhood gives you exceptional scope for understanding how your childhood shaped your behaviour as an adult. Alternately, the internet provides many articles on such a subject, which is well worth investigating.

Does all this make sense to you and how your foundations built your present?

CHAPTER 5

OK, So Where Do You Go From Here?

When they come back, remember how they left you.
- Sino Ako

As much as this man is the centre of your universe, given what you now know about your patterns in seeking the familiar in relationships (subconsciously), it is vital to begin thinking about yourself in healing 'you' from past trauma and gaining knowledge to positively affect your present and future. This knowledge may prevent you from ending up in a screaming heap over this affair, especially if you allow your current emotions to take hold, overwhelm and then consume you.

Is He Ever Going to Leave His Wife?

> To begin with, let's focus on the present and a writing exercise. Calm your mind and take a few slow, deep breaths. Then, using either paper and pen or a device, jot down some pros and cons about your situation. It is always helpful to unload your feelings and thoughts in this way because you are physically doing something practical to deal with your emotions.

By doing this, you not only organise and harness your thinking, but you also halve the pressure and turmoil inside your head by seeing and reading back what you have written. This helps you better understand what is happening within you.

First, make an emotions list. Use a few pages for this, and on the first page, write in bullet points how you felt before the turmoil happened – all the positive and wonderful feelings you had. How you felt each time you saw him, what it was about him that made you feel that way. There is no limit to the number of points you make; just write as much as you need to.

This will help you avoid staying stuck longing for him. If you just think about the good times you have lost, that's when your life spirals downward because you are only looking at one perspective of the whole. Yes, there were good things to remember. But the reality of what now has changed and how that will impact you are just as important.

On the second page, write down what changed within you when the bombshell hit. Be as descriptive and truthful as you can and let your emotions flow onto the page. By writing them

OK, So Where Do You Go From Here?

down, you are not only bringing up the negative emotions you are feeling but releasing them from within.

You can write one-word descriptions, if that is all you can manage, or write short descriptions of the feelings you experienced before and after – happy, bliss, delight, fulfilled, or rage, disappointment, betrayal, 'So help me, I am going to slice off his boy bits!'

On the third page, write down everything that has altered between you and this man, which is likely to affect your future now. Again, be as truthful as you can be; don't let how you feel about him cloud the truth. Include everything you can and cannot do about the situation and your views of where you stand at this point. For example, 'I am in two minds about him', 'I hate being lied to', 'I feel broken and betrayed', 'The trust I had in him is no longer there', 'This is going to impact my future', 'I have feelings towards him in that I still want to remove his nuts!'.

Once you are finished, cross out anything from this list you are not able to deal with – anything that is out of your control, like the fact he is married, and anything you are not sure of (your future together). You are then left with points you can manage, possibly take care of, and resolve (except for the physical violence – best leave that to his wife). By doing this, you are looking at the situation constructively and truthfully, and then you can decide what you can and cannot do for yourself with this man. Like I mentioned in the beginning, this is all about you now.

On another page, think about and write down everything you observed about him that you may have overlooked because you either were blinded by love or glossed over aspects of his behaviour. Your gut feeling may have indicated a possible red flag about him that wasn't as significant then, but now you can see how those 'little' things, once strung together, added up to this outcome. Do not blame yourself for not being able to understand those clues; you had no reason to doubt him.

When you take a step back and look at things from a focused perspective, you can see what didn't ring true. Like, why could he only see you on certain days or evenings? Why did he have to cancel your date that time? Why did he not want intimacy that night when he usually can't get you to the bedroom fast enough? Why didn't he talk about his life or himself other than work? That air of mystery you loved about him turned out to be him being secretive.

Of course, you took him at his word, and why wouldn't you? So, what were the gut feelings you ignored, but now looking back, things added up to him having another life away from you, and now everything falls into place? (You head for the kitchen to sharpen that knife!)

Writing down your thoughts and feelings may give you some clarity about what direction you feel you need to go, so give it a try. Help your emotions settle, organise your thoughts and lessen the effect of what happened to you.

Yes, you are in pain right now because a broken heart is an actual physical symptom, so be gentle with yourself over the next few days. Try and continue your normal routine, as hard as this may be, and focus on resuming and, better yet, rebuilding your life. This will be the key to recovery and moving forward.

CHAPTER 6

The Fallout

If you are in too deep with this man, there are some truths you need to reflect on now that your world has been fractured so directly.

You may first need to consider if you can even trust him. He kept a major secret about his life from you, so what will your future together be like? Is there anything else he is not telling you? It is not selfish or intrusive of you to want to know the details of his life, the agenda, the truth about his relationship with you and his wife, and how all this will impact your well-being and future; so be honest with yourself about this.

Women naturally think, reason and process situations differently than men. Our need to understand the details of a situation, especially when it will affect our lives and impact us directly, to comprehend the 'why' of something happening and figure out a solution is part of who we are.

You must wonder what then influenced his decisions and why he didn't tell you he was either married or in a permanent relationship at any point – from first developing that bond with you, which grew into being close friends, and finally blossoming into a steady relationship. There is nothing casual about this situation on your part. If you have been physically intimate with him for however long, then you have been in a 'relationship' with that man. Not only was he dishonest to his wife but to you as well. In hindsight, in a sense, you weren't really dating him; he was not your boyfriend, even though it felt that way, and he was not exclusive with you, which makes him deliberately deceitful and a liar.

Even by today's standards of love and having sex early on after meeting, having an affair is still considered a social taboo in anyone's language. He was completely fine with breaking your trust and another woman's. (Are the alarm bells beginning to sound in your head now?)

The first step in dealing with the emotions

In dealing with the fallout, your priority is to concentrate on being kind to yourself. If you meditate, then you are already equipped with being able to calm your mind and relax. Find a quiet place, sit comfortably, take some deep breaths, and allow the emotions to surface. If it helps, cry as much as it takes.

Dealing with your emotions at this early stage means you are preparing yourself to heal. If you need to wallow in this fractured state, then so be it. However, if you can, only allow a few days to detach from the world while gently dealing with these raw emotions. Then, before you make any decisions regarding ever

The Fallout

seeing him again or even speaking with him, if you have worked on your self, you will be better equipped to handle the next step.

If you are employed, go about your job with dignity, even though you are an emotional powder keg inside. If you find yourself having a screaming session with the office stapler, that is perfectly acceptable!

The time you have taken for yourself, without any contact with him, will be valuable for your emotional and mental well-being. Yes, you will miss him, and you won't be able to stop thinking about him, and that is perfectly understandable (and we will deal with that directly). But the last thing you want is to start a dialogue in your vulnerable state and for him to persuade you that being in his life while he is still married is a good thing. For him, maybe, but certainly not for you – neither now nor in the long run.

The temptation to contact him will be as strong as a junkie needing a fix because love is a drug, baby. No doubt you will get numerous calls and texts from him wanting to know if you are all right or if there's anything he can do, but please try hard to resist the urge to return contact unless you are mentally strong enough to make rational decisions without being swayed by him.

Your future with him and how well he will treat you if you take him back will be determined by this course of absence, making you calmer, clearer and stronger in what you want for yourself. You will not be deciding anything under pressure or from an emotional perspective, so take the time to build resistance and inner strength because your heart has already had all the battering it can take.

Is He Ever Going to Leave His Wife?

This time apart will also place you in a healthier position from within yourself but also with him, although it will certainly not feel like it. It is important you make it very clear to him that you are worth his respect and that you will not accept any further bad behaviour.

Don't worry, he is not going anywhere if that is what you are concerned about. Even though you might think you are abandoning him, know that he will be feeling your absence, which is a good thing because it gives him the opportunity to reflect on his actions and be aware of how he treats you. He may be a cheat, but if he has some decency, he will wait for you as you wished. If he doesn't, then you have your answer as to his integrity.

If you decide you want to see or speak to him, and you feel much stronger after the absence, then you have taken back your power. Think about what you will say, what you will accept and stick to your guns. As you already know, he is a charming manipulator, and two women you know of have fallen for that charm.

CHAPTER 7

OK, It's Truth Time

Before you meet or speak with him again, remember he was forced to reveal the truth about his married status. Now he will plead his case as to why he didn't tell you about this deal-breaker. His answer would be something in the nature of 'Because there was never a right time to tell you …' (OK, so he couldn't bring himself to say to you on your second date, between the entrée and the main course, that there was something you should know?)

When he was caught, however, he had no option but to appeal to your good nature. Because he knew full well that you love him deeply, he oozed as much sincerity and remorse as he could muster, hoping you would forgive him for this 'immense' secret he kept from you. He hoped, with a little persuasion, you could both continue where you left off. (Well, this is all about him, then!)

Is He Ever Going to Leave His Wife?

Be prepared for when he tells you how sorry he is, how much he adores you – no, 'loves you' more than life itself. If he could just take you in his arms and look into your beautiful eyes, then you would see just how sincere he is about you. Incidentally, didn't you have a great thing going together? (Yes, you did have a great thing going up until he was forced to admit to being a liar and a cheat – then all bets are off!)

Well, maybe if this were a romance novel where that sort of fiction happens, he might get away with it, but this is reality and it's your life he is playing with. There is so much emotion involved between you both at this moment. He sincerely does not want to lose you. Why? Because you are everything his wife isn't. Hang on, don't get too excited; it's not what you think. She has a history with him, while you are still fresh.

While your decision about letting him back into your life is going to be based on the truth, let's pause and look at things from his perspective and what motivated him to let a thing like being married just slide.

As it happened, you both met and fell in love. His home life with his wife was far from rosy. Whether he planned this or not, he jumped at the chance when he met someone he could be himself with, have fun with. Someone who could comprehend him and whom he could love and love him back without having to deal with the mundane side of family life.

The last thing you expected was for him not to be free to commit to you – but away from that for a minute. From his perspective, because he has genuine feelings for you and was afraid of your reaction to the 'married' part, there would have been, to a lesser degree, mounting anxiety and guilt each time he saw you. But he reasoned the situation with: If something is not broken, then why try and fix it?

As he began to fall in love with you – and yes, he did fall for you – it was clear to you both that something special was happening. He, then, opted for the 'need to know' tactic in your affair; if you were both happy, then 'You didn't need to know!' about the wife.

His dilemma, then, compounded as it became harder to tell you the deeper he got. The fear of losing you outweighed his honesty about his situation, so instead of manning up, he said nothing. Why? Because you were his fantasy romance, the perpetual great time with a beauty and body that stoked his ego. It would have been torture for him to leave you each time and go back to his 'existence' with the wife. But the moment he drove home, stark reality quickly brought him to earth, and his life with that woman inside – probably oblivious to anything happening between you – waited for him.

You can imagine his apprehension each time he walked in through their front door. Would she suspect anything? Could she smell you on him (that's why he took a shower just before he left)? Does he look guilty? Does he look too happy? If his wife does not know about his affair, then it is business as usual. But women are clever creatures, and they can sniff out a misdeed like a bloodhound on a scent. If she had a whiff about his infidelity, she would deck him!

There was a time when he once loved and adored her like he does you and willingly watched her walk down the aisle to him, made promises to each other, and were then pronounced husband and wife. However, as life wore on, he felt like he had been manacled to a ball and chain. So, what happened?

Something changed from the early days of love and a bright future together. It may have been any trigger that sowed the seeds of discontent. Still, for whatever reason, the restlessness and grind of daily life became a silent chasm between them. This is where you need to calmly discuss with him what happened for their marriage to have distorted this way.

Ask him how the relationship started to deteriorate. Has he spoken to his wife about the problems? What compelled him to take up with another woman? You need to stress that you want the truth (as he may embellish things a little). If he does verbalise their issues, it may help him see and understand what he needs to do to sort out these complications.

Be conscious of the red flags, however. Not everything will be her fault, and as the saying goes, 'It takes two to tango'! So, a word of warning here: Men in this situation will say anything if it means placing them in a good light. The truth, however, could be that he does not want to face the seriousness of his situation with you or his wife at home. This, then, lends itself to what issues he may be harbouring regarding what may have impacted him growing up. (Remember Chapter 4?)

Be aware that his wife will also have her side of things – most likely quite different from the version he will tell you. So, no matter how sincere he may sound and how sorry he may look, take it with a grain of salt for now. But have a heart-to-heart with him and see what he says (provided he is willing to discuss things with you of this nature, as he may not).

OK, It's Truth Time

What is your gut instinct telling you about him? Remember, he kept a secret from you that changes everything – from the relationship between you to how he treats you and conducts himself around you. (He's got to step up his game from now on!)

The following chapter will help you with his response to your questions. As they say, 'Fore-warned is fore-armed!'

CHAPTER 8

Throw Down the Gauntlet

If you are serious about wanting him to stay in your life, and he has given you good reason to anticipate him leaving his marital relationship and is willing to do what it takes to be with you, then honesty between you is essential. Make it clear to him what you will and won't accept in your relationship from now on. These few days of absence will make this conversation difficult but necessary.

Be clear about what you want him to do (leave his wife) and give him a time frame. Say, two months is ample. If he is serious about you and wants to end his marriage, he will agree and begin extricating himself from his wife. However, his true colours and any agenda he will have about why he is even with you will be disclosed at this point in the conversation. No doubt, he will immediately remind you of the reasons he can't leave his marriage and expect you to sympathise with him.

What he says next will determine your course of action, and the next three scenarios will help you understand what to expect with each.

Please Note: The following sections can be confronting, and while it is not my intention to cause you pain, I will be honest with you.

Scenario One: He's a user

If he tells you he thought you were fine with remaining as friends (with benefits), then you have your answer as to his integrity and how he sees you in this relationship. Despite your love for him, understand this affair is all about him, his needs, his happiness and releasing his frustration with you. (Don't, for one second, think you are special because he's with you. With a man like that, it simply isn't so!)

With this scenario, he just has designs on using you for his own gratification. These are brutal and soul-destroying words to read, I know, and I am sorry. But the reality now may save you even more heartbreak.

If he begins making excuses for delaying or deferring to leave his wife, then the plain truth is that you are nothing more than a distraction and a convenience for him when **he** needs you – and that's not fair on you. This is by no means the type of relationship built on honesty, and it will not develop into anything more than the lust he feels towards you because it certainly is not love, and things between you will remain this way for as long as you keep it so.

Think about how this lifestyle will impact you and your mental health five, ten years from now (if you last that long). Men like him are only interested in what they can get from the woman they are having an affair with. When the relationship wears down (as they always do – look at his marriage) or when things get complicated, especially when you start to want more from the relationship, he will bail on you. To him, there will always be other women who will give him what he wants without the complications he already has at home with his wife. He does not want a repeat performance with anyone else.

Meanwhile your biological clock is ticking

If you want to have your own children, chances are, it won't happen with him because that is not in his plan. He just wants an uncomplicated good time. Any thoughts you might harbour about deliberately falling pregnant with him may catastrophically backfire. You forced him into a situation he does not want to be in, so if this is the course you may be contemplating, then think about the side of him you might not be prepared for.

Suppose you do happen to fall pregnant, then no matter his views, the legalities in place will make him take responsibility for the child regardless of whether he wants to or not and whether he decides to stay married. (Ha! Wouldn't you just love to be a fly on the wall when that conversation detonates with his wife? 'Oh, and by the way, honey, the Other Woman I am sleeping with behind your back is pregnant!')

After she clocks him with a frying pan, know that you may have no future with him whatsoever because you took away his choices and control, and his disdain for you will be long remembered (so will his black eye!).

If he is self-absorbed (probably a narcissist by character), he will certainly be indifferent to your needs. So, this will be a solitary road for you to walk. Understand he only cares for himself and what impacts him, so the quicker you are out of the equation, the better. Too many red flags with this one, honey!

Scenario Two: He's open to the possibilities

He wants to be with you but doesn't know how to leave (for whatever reason). This is where you can calmly talk with him and help form a strategy to exit his situation.

There may be some resistance from him at first (fear of the unknown), but his body language will change to indicate an open, relaxed posture. He may lean towards you with total focus and remain calm even when talking about his anxieties around leaving. These are all positive signs. As the conversation progresses, if he begins to show enthusiasm about making this next step happen with you, chances are he is serious about wanting to leave his wife.

The proof will be if, over the next few days or weeks, he begins to act on the plans you discussed with each other. He's serious when he makes an appointment with a divorce lawyer, moves out, doesn't care if you are both seen in public together, and no longer keeps you a secret. This is a great outcome, and he is someone who values you, genuinely wants to be with you, and appreciates your patience and understanding during his exit.

You may also be in for a bumpy ride, as his wife won't be thrilled about losing her husband to another woman. If she is anything like the horror he described, then brace yourself – unless she is happy to be well rid of him, then 'Yay, you!'

Scenario Three: He wants out, but there is too much at stake to pack a bag and leave

In discussing this with you, he weighs the situation carefully, and all sorts of consequences keep coming up. What if the kids no longer want to speak to him? What if the wife takes everything in the divorce? What will his parents, friends or work colleagues say? (Odds on, he is already weighing the outcome of this catastrophe waiting to happen!)

The more he loses, the more he will think twice about leaving her. This is really a difficult decision he must make. If he has spent years building a home, a life, a career and a status, then getting out of that is a bit like walking on broken glass through a minefield. It will be painful and messy no matter how much care he takes.

It is all very well for him to think he can have a great life and be happy with you, and one day he might, but there are issues to be resolved and many factors to consider larger than he is presently prepared for. So, for now, there is a lot at stake for him to face, and you must be patient (to an extent), keep to your word and handle him with special care.

If, as in the second scenario, he begins to dissolve things with his wife – even though it may take time – and proves he is genuine about you, wants to make a future with you and works

Is He Ever Going to Leave His Wife?

to make it happen, then great! Go be happy together when it is finally resolved.

BUT if you then start to see the stalling and delays because, for whatever reason he comes up with, it is too difficult to leave 'his life', then take it that this is too much for him. The likelihood of him going through with this will be zero.

It may not be because he does not want to but because he is stuck and overwhelmed and leaving her is impossible. He doesn't have what it takes to go through with it, but he doesn't want to lose you either and keeps you hanging (except, him not leaving her is him not leaving her).

Take inspiration from the song
'Keep Me Hangin' On' by Kim Wild

CHAPTER 9

Moving On Today

In the above three scenarios, you will handle the situation according to his response. With each, a different plan needs to be implemented and acted upon.

If, in the first scenario, he insists that you are either his mistress or else he moves on to another set of fresh sheets, then you will seriously need to give what he told you honest thought and decide if you will be happy in that type of life with him. Be true to yourself when considering if your self-esteem is so low that you will keep a man like that at any cost.

Women who lie to themselves and pretend it will all work out cannot accept the reality of the situation with their married man. Chances are, with this first scenario, things between you may not work out – you are worth a better life and much more happiness than you are getting. You just need the courage to allow yourself to have that and begin taking responsibility for yourself to get it.

Could you be the Mistress?

Some women, however, remain completely satisfied with having their own life and him being the icing on the cake. She loves that he showers her with gifts – expensive or otherwise (anything from paying for dinner or groceries to him seeing to the rent and utilities are paid for; some even have an apartment or car gifted to them).

The fact he is married is neither here nor there because she is a separate issue and keeps it that way. Their affair will not affect his relationship with his wife. She is happy to see him when he calls around because she has her own life and is confident in herself not wanting anything more.

This is not, by any means, a bad thing, especially if you know your worth, are self-assured and prefer to have the life you choose without complications (she takes responsibility for her 'self' and well-being). If that is you, then all power to you, and this book may not be for you. Regardless, you go, girl!

So, if he does end up leaving his wife for you, then the battle is half over (Notice I said **half** over?). Setting up a domestic life with you is one thing; dealing with the destruction of his other life is something else entirely. So, let the games begin!

There will be fallout and wreckage no matter what he does, because a woman will fight dirty to keep her man despite her feelings for him – and they will change from feelings of love to utter contempt in a millisecond. If she, then, knows he is leaving her for you, then watch her turn into full-fury tsunami mode, creating total devastation in her wake with the intent of causing him as much hurt, disruption, chaos and mayhem as possible – financially, socially and within the family – for not just betraying her but because of the hell he is putting her (and possibly the kids) through. Whether deserved or not, all is fair in love and war!

You both will have to deal with some nasty stuff originating from her (and eventually her lawyers) and, understandably, from anyone who takes her side. What's more, they will close ranks with her against you both. Make no mistake; when things get ugly, this will feel like a battle to the death now that the lines have been drawn.

At this time, he will need a lot of support and encouragement. Even though you may be strong enough to resist the barrage of anger about to descend because you do not have a history with her, he will probably feel her wrath substantially more.

What will be going through his mind?

There would be a lot of uncertainty and doubt about what his actions will do to the kids and the woman he married. This is not coming from a place of regret but compassion towards his family for the suffering he could be inflicting, especially on the children. Still, if life with his wife were as bad as he described, then his remorse would be short-lived.

This is where you need to keep your cool and be gentle with him because, firstly, you are the better woman. Secondly, when

Is He Ever Going to Leave His Wife?

he sees how understanding you are regarding his moodiness or silence or even a change in character while he deals with the dross, he will soon acknowledge and accept why he is going through this upheaval and turmoil in the first place – to be with you.

This turbulent transition for both of you is to be expected, and you will equally have a lot to deal with all at once. So, plan to ease this passage for him by remaining neutral. Don't badmouth his wife, ever, and try not to 'put your oar in'! Instead, support him, comfort him and talk with him when he needs to, but let him deal with ending things with her. Even if she is bringing Armageddon upon him, he can only deal with one woman ushering in the apocalypse.

Also, if you keep pressing him at this time, it will put more pressure on him. Questioning everything he does, even though you are supporting and defending your man, is not what he needs. Perhaps, just calmly say, 'Honey, as hard as this is, it will all pass. You will both heal and be able to move on; just trust that this is a process and know I am here for you.'

Try to remain as calm and supportive as you can. He would be different with you for a while until he sorts everything out, but do not take it to heart, as it is the fallout of his decision catching up with him. This situation is not going to last forever.

Reassure him, be kind to yourself and him, talk things through and let him know that you're his girl if he needs a shoulder to lean on or a sounding board for the way forward! Do not react negatively to his off days or his confused outbursts, as he is trying to process all he is receiving and reacting to what is happening. Remember, this is currently all about him and

Moving On Today

what he is experiencing (not you), so keep this in mind and just go with the flow but under no circumstance accept any abuse from him. NONE!

The storm will pass. Once he has left the marriage, his ex will eventually get on with her life and the kids will adjust, especially if they see their father happy with you (and you are great with his kids). By presenting a safe and happy environment, the kids will want to spend time with you both.

It will take time and patience, but he is worth it. So, when it happens, and you are both free to devote yourselves to each other, go and build your life with the man of your dreams. You deserve every bit of happiness together.

CHAPTER 10

You Can Try and Change His Mind

As I mentioned in the third scenario in Chapter 8, if he is resisting to leave the marriage like a barnacle stuck on a whale, there are some things you can try to change his mindset.

You have already tried talking with him and offered solutions to his doubts, but he persists with 'I love you. You know I love you, but ... I can't leave my *wife*.'

Let's make no mistake here; what he is really saying to you is, 'I Can't Leave My **Life**'

That's it in a nutshell. He cannot seem to leave his established life despite his professing love for you. So, what to do about it? First, you must think about how this will impact your long-term future. This may be hard for you, but you will have to make this all about you and the happiness and life **you** deserve!

Below are some important strategies you can implement straight away.

You are going to stop sleeping with him.

Tell him in calm, plain language that while he remains with his wife, you are off limits until he leaves her. (Yes, I told you it may be hard, but it's not impossible.)

He may be shocked or smug in thinking you won't last without the passion between you, but either way, there is good reason for you doing this. If you detach from him physically, it will be easier to detach from him emotionally if one day you must, but keep to your word. If his love for you is real, then going without having you is truly going to test that sincerity, and he will give serious thought as to whether what he is staying for is worth it compared to losing you.

Let him know this affair is not going to go on indefinitely.

It is important for him to understand that he has a time limit, in which he either decides to act or it is over. This is perfectly reasonable because he needs to take responsibility for himself and choose what life he wants. Two months is ample time for him to do what he needs to and get the ball rolling out of his relationship. Make it clear that you cannot be with him again if he does not leave the marriage by then.

You Can Try and Change His Mind

You cannot take him at his word.

You need proof that he is really doing something about leaving. How would you know for sure he is not lying to you? By the end of the two months, he needs to provide proof of his sincerity by ending things with his wife – like moving out of the family home (preferably not with you), setting up a life away from her or starting divorce proceedings.

Limit your contact with him.

This will be the hardest for you, but if you want him to know you are serious about him keeping his word to you, then don't answer his phone calls, texts or whatever means you use to speak to each other. Instead, leave at least a few hours or even a day or so before you get back to him. This gives him a clear message that he is not your priority unless he leaves his wife.

When you do answer him, keep things very simple and short. Be pleasant, but only answer what he has asked and nothing more. It is not avoiding him or being rude. You're just looking after yourself first and making it clear that unless his priorities change, then yours will remain the same.

This is a clever move on your part; it allows you to begin working on yourself and doing what is right for you as well as keeping him from having the best of both worlds with you and his wife in the same picture.

Do not tell his wife.

This is a bad, bad move here (more on that later). Just don't do it!

You need to give him a clear message.

While he is still with his wife, you cannot be fully committed or invested in the relationship. It is not fair that you live in hope and he keeps you hanging. Once he leaves his wife, then you can be devoted to him – but not before.

Your girlfriends, family and work colleagues do not need to know.

As much as you love them and want to share details of your life with them, saying anything about your affair may backfire. If you have told them there is a man in your life, then leave it at that.

There is a good reason not to elaborate. Once you tell them he is married, their true colours become evident. There is a stigma attached to 'him' playing around on his wife and 'you' being taken as a fool. Even if none of that is true, people will judge you both as such. The less said, the better. Your besties will stick with you through thick and thin, but save them the worry for now.

If nothing has happened nearing the two-month deadline.

Start dating other single men, not to make him jealous (huge mistake) but because you are not exclusive with him (like he supposedly is with his wife). By seeing other people, you open the scope of finding a man who is available, treats you the way you deserve, makes you happy and is totally committed to you. Make it clear to your married man that he either makes a permanent commitment to you or lets you go.

You are not two-timing him, playing games, trying to manipulate him or forcing him to be with you. You have a right to find your own happiness. Take things slow and give yourself some breathing space, as this is not a rebound situation. If your married man does not like it, well, he knows what he needs to do.

Keep yourself looking great.

This is a win-win for you. By looking after yourself and looking and feeling your best, your self-worth, self-esteem, mental health and general well-being will grow. It's a domino effect; the better you like yourself and how you look, the more positive you are about yourself, your life and how you accept people treating you. This is you taking responsibility for yourself and acting for the best on your behalf.

Reassure him that you still want to be with him.

Let him know you still love him deeply, but you will not be the Other Woman. You are worth more than that. Be kind

Is He Ever Going to Leave His Wife?

and gentle but firm on this point because you are the most important person in this relationship for him and for you.

CHAPTER 11

What If You Already Know He Is Married?

If you are having an affair with this man and knew he was married before agreeing to the relationship, then there had been a point where you decided he was worth this lifestyle.

Some women are so completely in love with their married man that they care only about their next meeting. It is like being in a constant state of anticipatory bliss. The moment he turns up, you pick up where you left off. Both of you are in a state of ecstasy at seeing one another, and he is as besotted with you as you are with him.

It's like being in high school all over again, waiting to see and be with your crush. Except now, he has baggage a whole world away – a world you are not part of by design, but you know his family is there, and he returns to them after spending these precious moments with you.

Maybe you are satisfied with your life with him, and maybe it does not matter that he steals time away from his family to be with you. After all, you are both happy, and he says he loves you. If you are living the life you want, are treated well by him, fully understand his reason for not leaving his marriage – because it is a reason and not an excuse – and are not intimidated in any way by his family, then no one has any right to judge you.

Society, overall, is not forgiving when it comes to a woman seeing a married man. Yet, that same culture is more forgiving when the roles are reversed and a married woman is seeing an unattached man. The expressions you have undoubtedly heard – home wrecker, adulterer, back stabber (and they get worse from there) – stem primarily from religious and sociocultural beliefs that seep into the fabric of society and close ranks against the 'woman' – married or otherwise.

Here's the twist: some wives know about the Other Woman and accept this arrangement, as not all wives will be screaming banshees when they discover their husband's private life. These women have everything they've ever wanted – a husband, a family, a house, security and a great life – and know their husband loves them even though he sleeps with another.

They may not be completely happy with the arrangement. But if it means they get to keep their life, they overlook the indiscretion because they reason, 'He always comes back to me.' In that, they have a sense of tolerance and understanding.

What If You Already Know He Is Married?

These wives do not ask about their husband's Other Woman. They do not want to know anything about her, and if it is not discussed (rubbing her nose in it), and the Other Woman is a permanent liaison, then the wife can tolerate that part of their marriage. Especially if the wife does not have to engage in intimacy with him, she is happy to leave that to the Other Woman. If he is not kerb-crawling, then at some level, his wife is in accord with the affair because she knows who he is with and why.

He, no doubt, genuinely loves his wife. He also loves the woman he spends time with on weekends, other days and holidays. So, this understanding between the married couple sees their time together more akin to being housemates. They remain amicable, friends even, but as they enjoy different things, go out with different people and are responsible for their own happiness, an affair is not the earth-shattering, heart-breaking issue.

As I have mentioned earlier, all affairs are not born equal and neither are relationships, for that matter. As dating young adults, ideas may have been far different from the reality we face today in our relationships. If something works for you, makes you glad and fulfils your life without hurting yourself or anyone else, then you do what makes you both happy. If you have love, respect, growth and happiness in your relationship, then you deserve every bit of it. The rest of the world will one day catch up!

CHAPTER 12

The Polyamory Relationship

There will, of course, be exceptions to every marriage, especially when it is all but in name. The couple both have a life away from each other but stay married out of convenience and are happy to share a house, grown-up children, friends and the security of the marriage. They have separate lives and even discreetly see other people and prefer that lifestyle rather than divorce. Unconventional? Yes, but it works for them.

These couples have mostly been in long-term relationships. Through mutual understanding, the married man, then, finds another woman who completes his life and takes up an occasional relationship with her. The wife may do the same, but both the husband and wife make it clear to their attachments that they will not leave their marriage.

Is He Ever Going to Leave His Wife?

They're well-adjusted, caring and compassionate people who simply lack the intimacy they once shared with each other. For whatever reason, they look externally for that intimate side of their relationship. They are both understanding of each other's needs and know they still love each other, so what happens in Vegas stays in Vegas.

Theirs may be described as an open marriage – or polyamory. Younger couples today sometimes opt for this arrangement of casually seeing other people while married because they do not consider their marriage to conform to social, religious or cultural beliefs.

Yes, society takes a dim view of this type of freedom because society, marriage and family are based on upholding values that support the rearing of children in a secure, stable and happy home with two faithful parents. Step away from that established view, and the seeds of anarchy are sown. *Vive la difference!*

For a younger couple, the polyamory relationship is based on trust (and massive amounts of it). As long as there is equality in that trust, and they stick to the 'rules' of engagement in their infidelity (Is that an oxymoron?), their marriage is free from jealousy, secrets and lies of a conventional marriage in trouble. This arrangement works if the partners agree to the conditions – make it casual and do not fall in love.

Yeah, good luck with that. So tell me again, why did you guys get married?

Oh, to be with each other forever – but not exclusively so!

The Polyamory Relationship

So how does that work when kids come along? (Kids are always game changers)

Oh, you both don't want kids. Well, go your hardest!

In a healthy relationship, both people are well-adjusted, confident and secure within themselves and in each other, communicate well with their partner, work together as a team and constructively resolve issues. In short, they have a strong relationship. The dynamics change, however, when another party (or parties) comes permanently into the mix, whether it be a love interest or the birth of a child.

It makes sense that human beings need to find a way to live a life of happiness and fulfilment with a partner whose attitude towards marital freedom conform with theirs. This allows a stronger scope for their mental health to flourish and free them from the guilt that society places if they stray or opt for a polyamory relationship.

This is all well and good when there are no other issues to put a spanner in the works. However, things go from happy to hell on earth as quick as a race car goes from zero to 100 in under 60 seconds. While the idea of an open marriage may sound great to begin with and may work for the couple of funsters, the challenges that may eventuate – like having or not having children, other jealous parties or the onset of insecurity – could become serious issues, which are unique to the situation and must be approached and dealt with carefully. (A bit like stopping a hand grenade from going off when you've lost the pin – you either have to keep holding on to that sucker or throw it well away!)

Is He Ever Going to Leave His Wife?

Polyamory relationships can work for a while, but the marriage begins to change. The couple either stops seeing other people and concentrates on building a life together, realising how much they mean to each other. Or, the marriage ends because the complications of having an open marriage come to light. As much as they may both initially agree to have this type of relationship, jealousy may be the factor to break them.

This begs the question of whether they really were devoted to and loved each other enough to withstand the influences of external relationships. They would need to be strong, independent people who were secure enough in themselves and each other for this type of relationship to work. Who knows? Religion and culture aside, this may well be how marriage will look in the future – although we are a long way from that type of freedom.

CHAPTER 13

Why Men Cheat

This is a biggie! To understand why men cheat, we must first look at what drives them to do so. There can be a myriad of excuses and reasons as to why men seek outside intimacy, and their method of choice could range from an online hook-up to full-blown relationships with one or more women. So, why do they do it?

If you strip away the onion, you are left with a man unhappy with his life or a crisis happening either outwardly or within him. He could look to another woman for solace because confiding in his wife may make him look weak and ineffectual. He may even feel he has to justify his worth to himself or try to make up for the shortcomings in his life, so he looks to another woman.

If a married man is unhappy with his marital situation – say, being unhappily tied to one woman – then his wife will never measure up no matter what she does for him. He loses interest in her and looks elsewhere for excitement, pleasure, fulfilment, challenge or revenge. He is always in search of external justification to satisfy his internal lack. This all stems from the foundations instilled, perhaps, during his upbringing, resulting in how he views himself as an adult.

The thrill of the chase, the excitement of conquest and the pride in himself for getting away with juggling two separate and mostly secret lives are exhilarating. It gives him the opportunity to live out a real-life fantasy. This behaviour is a red flag as to what is going on within him. What he's really doing is looking for answers for the fulfilment he lacks and has been battling with this deficiency, probably, from childhood. He is not equipped to deal with or understand his dilemma, especially if he has no idea there is even a problem or that one ever existed. His inability to resolve matters in adulthood, especially with his wife or partner, means he is stuck in that immaturity.

The One-Night Stand

His affairs may start out as an unplanned, opportunistic one-night stand. He meets a woman, and they end up sharing a hotel room. For him, there will be no emotion attached to this act – just a physical attraction to a body, a release to give him a momentary thrill in an intoxicating and insubstantial way.

He may continue in this manner, having one-night stands any time a crisis emerges because his method of operation is to deal with things superficially. This crisis could be as trifle as having an argument with his wife or boss or getting a speeding ticket. Either way, he lacks the maturity to assess and take responsibility for his reaction.

A string of one-night stands, and he becomes a serial cheater, a womaniser, unless he opts for a more permanent relationship with another woman. In any case, there are issues he is unwilling or unable to deal with. Even though he knows and justifies what he is doing, he is willing to jeopardise his future with his wife. But, he knows his wife well enough to calculate the risks and enjoy both worlds he has created because he simply lacks the capacity to devote himself to either woman.

While the pretence remains intact – wife, home, children, work, friends – an affair is the ideal way of coping and dealing with his frustrations. The Other Woman provides a sympathetic ear and understands him, 'unlike his wife'. (If he says this to you, take it with a grain of salt and the first red flag.)

Instead of upsetting the applecart and dispensing with the problem head-on, like any well-adjusted man does, he blames everyone else – but especially his wife or boss, any authority, or the world in general – for all his misery. So, he has an affair. (This may point to narcissistic behaviour and a second red flag!)

He develops a lifelong pattern where relationships always start out happy, amicable, exciting and fun – even loving and meaningful. But as soon as the honeymoon period is over – six months to two years – the staleness sets in when issues arise. It begins to eat away at him, and the pattern of dissatisfaction starts all over again (Red flag number three!). If he is unhappy within himself and has cheated with you on his wife, there is every chance he will do so with you as well; just give it time. (That's three strikes, buddy!)

Is He Ever Going to Leave His Wife?

*Take inspiration from the song
'My Bad Habits Lead To You' by Ed Sheeran*

Revenge Cheating

There is another form of an affair known as revenge cheating. This is where one partner is so angry at his spouse and so frustrated by her indifference to him that he gets revenge by deliberately finding a woman to have sex with and put him back together. His is an affair with an agenda, so he justifies sex with another woman to get back at his wife in the most damaging way.

He is not only angry at his spouse and himself, but he's also angry at breaking the vows they once held to mean something. He feels betrayed by a marital system that has trapped them in an unrealistic life, so he breaks her trust out of spite and defiance.

The cheating partner may opt to let the cat out of the bag as to his indiscretion. Thus, deliberately hurting the wife in a game of tit-for-tat (you hurt me, so now I'm hurting you). Or, he may just walk in through the front door as if nothing happened, knowing his secret can be used as a weapon one day. Either way, by not being able to deal with the problems he faces within himself, especially if he is unable to talk with his wife about what is troubling him, their troubles will be ongoing and their marriage unhealthy.

It is a huge leap from acknowledging a problem within him to realising his internal flaw and wanting to do something about it. Suppose, however, he begins to take responsibility for his pattern of behaviour, admits his dissatisfaction within himself and understands there is a reason why he repeats this pattern. Then, with professional help, he will go a long way to breaking that cycle and reaching true happiness with the woman he loves.

The Dark Side

A word of warning: While this book deals specifically with a married man having an affair, there poses a genuine danger within any relationship wherein a person is unable to deal with the pressures of their life productively and maturely. Their response is to lash out and resort to violence. They may have deep-seated, negative issues that have never been addressed or resolved, which distorts their reality and any chance of a healthy relationship.

When a person chooses to take out their frustrations on their partner – and even their kids – no amount of justification and remorse afterwards will ever absolve them of their actions. They either need to seek professional help if they acknowledge their mental issue or their victim must protect themselves with external help. Period!

Other men, however, side-step their issues by having affairs. Both scenarios are damaging in different ways yet may stem from deep-seated problems – their inability to deal with these issues has manifested in avoidance behaviour. No matter the excuse, whether it is their 'nature' (ingrained in their DNA) or how they were 'nurtured' (their environment or upbringing), there may be flaws within them that lead to violence. It is **never** OK to abuse a woman or children.

CHAPTER 14

All Narcissists Are Not Created Equal

This is a covert condition until it becomes apparent to the victim. Most people, if asked what they think a narcissist is, will tell you they are a person who has a very high opinion of themselves. In its simplest form, they would be correct, but that barely scratches the surface; narcissism has a more sinister side.

Why am I telling you this? Most men who have affairs fall into two categories. Either they are so frustrated with themselves and their life that they need to seek an outlet for their stifled existence, or there is the possibility they may have a degree of narcissism and need that external veneration despite the relationship with their wife.

Narcissistic Types

Narcissists can be the most charming assassins. Their beguiling ways soon have you falling for them but soon transform once they have you in their clutches. They fall into a few basic categories[1], which can be basically broken down as follows:

The Covert or Vulnerable Narcissist

The Covert Narcissist is the least recognisable of all narcissistic types. They are contrary to typical narcissistic behaviour. They do not desire the focus and attention typical narcissists do. Instead, they are diffident, modest, hypochondriacs and hypersensitive to how others see them. Despite this, they crave compliments, and an affair boosts their self-image. But despite evidence to the contrary, they are primarily the centre of their universe.

The Cerebral Narcissist

Not necessarily nerds per se, but this type of narcissism is derived from their intelligence and intellect. Because they believe they are smarter than everyone else, they are constantly impatient with people, to the point of arrogance. They see everyone else as intellectually inferior to them and are full of their own importance (and usually have the personality of a dial tone!).

All Narcissists Are Not Created Equal

The Somatic Narcissist

Somatic Narcissists are the nasty gym junkies – shallow as a teaspoon and see their bodies as much to be envied in their perfection. They get their fix and self-worth by obsessing over their appearance. As they are constantly at a physical peak, everyone else is judged and criticised by whether they measure up in appearance. (These guys need tweezers to hold their cashew to pee!)

The Spiritual Narcissist

(Gods, give me strength.) Spiritual Narcissists use their religious beliefs to terrorise or harm others they consider not as holy as they are. Their fundamental belief somehow gives them an advantage because they think they are closer to God. They imagine a direct connection to Him, which can place them into the pathological category.

The Sympathy Narcissist

This element of narcissism thrives from gaining your sympathy. They always seem to suffer from being broken in some way, whether by others or by a full-blown illness (real or imaginary). And because they get their kicks from people feeling sorry for them, they will do and say anything to get mileage from this; the worse their condition, the more they are suffering, the more you will be taken in.

While you will naturally sympathise with their sad condition, be careful here. This person may play you. They are master manipulators, and in their twisted way, their control comes from seeing you emotionally stricken for them.

A Narcissist in Brief

You will not know at first if you are involved with a narcissist because he is charming and magnetic. He understands how to lay on the appeal to make you feel like the most special person in the world. He showers you with flowers and gifts, compliments, love texts and little touches of his admiration, and you can't help but fall for such a romantic guy. This is the love bombing phase.[2]

He oozes confidence, personality and appeal, and the exhilaration of being with him makes other men pale in comparison. He is a unique man, and you love everything about him. He thrives on being around you and adores your attention and approval; everything is fantastic in your relationship. (So why isn't he already taken?)

As the relationship progresses, however, you notice changes in him; traits that, when put together, spell out something different from what he first portrayed. You find, perhaps, he has an inflated ego and exaggerates his sense of self-worth. He makes sure you know how super intelligent he thinks he is and how he is always the single-handed hero in some drama and often overstates his achievements and talents.

He has always talked big and has big plans to make himself rich and change the world. He big-notes himself with a demanding air, which feeds his need for admiration. He loves being the centre of attention and being told how special he is, which further feeds his ego – the centre of his being.

All Narcissists Are Not Created Equal

A narcissistic person expects special treatment from everyone, especially adoration – even reverence – from you. Have you noticed how self-centred and vain he is and how he takes over conversations that tend to end up about him? You begin to see how he now talks down to people and shows a lack of empathy, even taking advantage of them and is generally arrogant and dismissive of others.[1]

He does not take criticism well because he lacks the capacity to understand what is really going on with people, so if he is ever put in his place by someone, not only do they become the enemy but the problem always lies with them and never with him. He becomes preoccupied with his sense of authority, success and anything that will make him look superior and is hell-bent on holding you back from what you want to achieve. God forbid you are better than him in any way.

He has drawn you in, and before you realise the extent of your fit-up, you are trapped – caught like a butterfly in his web. This is when you become familiar with his darkness, his true character, and the evil within him comes to light. You find he is quick to anger and has trouble keeping calm if contradicted. He intimidates you and exerts control, even gaslights you (more on that later). So, you are always alert to his mood and seem to continually walk on eggshells around him. (Soul-destroying behaviour)

The longer you are with him, your mental health, self-confidence and self-esteem eventually erode. You then start doubting yourself, and that's when he begins to isolate you from friends and family. This is a dangerous phase because you are being trapped, manipulated, taken advantage of, taken over and made dependent on him before completely being consumed emotionally by this creep.

Is He Ever Going to Leave His Wife?

You cringe when he belittles someone he considers fair game because it is like a sport to him. You, then, understand how he has problems with relationships, work and financial matters, having difficulty relating to and understanding the needs and feelings of others.[3]

If you identify these qualities in your man, I have three words for you: GET OUT FAST!

Take inspiration from the song
'Somebody That I Used to Know'
by Gotye and Kimbra

CHAPTER 15

Narcissistic Behaviour and How It Affects You

A Narcissist doesn't break your heart, they break your spirit.
That's why it takes so long to heal.

Below is a list of common traits associated with this insidious characteristic. If you recognise any of these traits in the man you are seeing, take this as a wake-up call for you to either cut and run or seek professional help for yourself, even if it is speaking with your doctor. These are not healthy mental traits in a person, and they will eventually become damaging to you. With prolonged exposure to these behaviours and tactics, you will pay the price one way or another. No man is worth losing your sanity or your life over.

Breadcrumbing

He sends out non-committal but clearly definitive signals that he is interested in you, setting out the trail of breadcrumbs for you to follow before he snares you. Then, he gives you just enough attention to make you want more, but he never fully commits.[4] (Loser!)

Gaslighting

He manipulates you by making what he said and did as something you are taking out of proportion or context. He makes it so you are the one with the problem by saying things like 'Don't be so sensitive; it was only a joke' or making you think you are paranoid or constantly confusing you so that you doubt your own reality.[5] (He is the one who has several screws loose, not you!)

Superiority Complex

A true indication of his character is how he treats people he encounters, especially those in humble positions. Is he rude to them or treats them with contempt? Looks and talks down to them or is outright offensive? He sees himself as superior to everyone, including you![6] (Super Creep!)

Zombieing

First, he ghosts you after breaking up with you. Then, out of the blue, he reappears and wants to revive the relationship

– probably because there is no better offer.[6] (Nothing for months from this man, and suddenly he's back from the dead!)

Benching

He leaves you waiting on the bench, not quite committed to you but also not wanting to let you go in case someone else shows interest in you.[6] (Seriously, dude, just grow a pair!)

Stonewalling

You get the complete shutdown treatment. He refuses to communicate with you, thus stonewalls you. No matter what you say to him or how you try and coax him into communicating, you get nothing. He is present with you but non-communicative.[7] (Immature Jerk!)

Passive Aggressive

Passive aggressive people show their anger by withholding something they know you want through procrastination, stubbornness and obstructionism. Or, they give you a backhanded compliment, usually laced with sarcasm[8] – 'Didn't you say you were on a diet? So, no dessert for you if you want to fit into that dress. But I'll have the chocolate chip chocolate cake with extra chocolate.' (Stay the hell away from this one!)

Repeat Victim

Every woman he has ever been involved with has treated him badly and broken his heart. He is a repeat victim who wants to tell you, in detail, about each heartbreak.[6] (He loves sympathy and will say the same thing about you one day to someone else!)

Covert Conspirator

He will, at some stage, use whatever you tell him, especially in confidence, against you. Or, he will try to influence or control you by twisting what you said and keeping it as ammunition against you.[6] (Vengeful Jerk!)

User and Abuser

This narcissistic trait of a user and abuser means he will take advantage of you or anyone you know if he has something to gain from it without a second thought about how this could impact that person or damage you.[1] (No moral compass means no moral compunction to ever treat you well.)

Twisted Praising

He **only** praises you when you are both with someone else, so they witness him being a great guy. Then he begins to overdo compliments to others close to you – a backhanded way of reinforcing any insecurity about yourself.[9] (Next time he does that, call him a *cashew*!)

Cheater

Are you surprised narcissists are likely to cheat on their wives, given what you now know? It's all about feeding their ego and inflating their sense of self. Those narcissistic men who cheat on their wives tend to repeat the same patterns with every woman they become involved with – she never measures up, and when they break up, it is always her fault.[10] (A few choice names come to mind, but none I can repeat in print!)

Comparison Critic

He does this to hurt you and deliberately flirts with another woman in front of you or compares you to an ex or the other woman he is flirting with.[9] (And you want to stay with this jackass?)

Deflective Deceiver

If he knows your family and sees you are having trouble coping with what he is doing to you, he will use that against you by telling them he is concerned about you because you are not yourself. The family would think, *What a caring guy.* This tactic deflects any blame away from him, so you are the one who has the problem.[9] (Get the hell away from him FAST!)

Devious Isolator

You are systematically cut off from friends and family.[9] He is a nasty piece of work because he manipulates you in a way that systematically cuts you off from everyone, making sure you have no support network. (Three red flags, honey. Pack a bag and RUN!)

Contempt Monger

Your needs are important. It is also important to talk about your needs and feelings for your own mental health and well-being. But if you are met with apathy, indifference, disgust or sarcasm, he clearly holds you in contempt.[11] (So, why are you with this low-life punk?)

Strategic Defensiveness

Tied in with gaslighting, you always seem to be defending yourself somehow. Whether it is trying to explain your actions or reactions, you are always having to justify or defend yourself.[11] (You need to drop this dude, like, NOW!)

Keeping Tabs

He keeps tabs on you, and at first it looks caring, but then it escalates to something else entirely, like who you can see or are 'allowed' to be with when you're away from him. He will raise objections about your people ALWAYS! He opens your mail, looks at your phone to see whom you are talking to or texting, and is constantly gathering information and stalking you (which is illegal). He does this supposedly for your own good.[6] (Condescending little man! Who does he think he is?)

Closeted Woman Hater

Watch out for this one. He's a lovely guy, but then he catches you off guard with how he talks about other women. He is discourteous and treats them just as bad as his opinions of them.[6] (Give it time, honey. He will treat you the same way!)

Unbalanced Favours

To him, the scales must always be in his favour. If he does something for you – and makes a big deal about it – then you better be grateful. Not only that, but he expects above and beyond from you in return, and you better make it snappy![6] (So, he's self-centred, conceited and insincere!)

Deliberate Baiting

He deliberately sets you up by baiting you for a fight, and it is all your fault for fighting with him.[6] (What an angry, bitter and twisted little man. So you are with him, why?)

Super Nice Guy

He is a wolf in sheep's clothing because he pretends to be this sweet and agreeable man, but he is a faker. He uses his niceness with an agenda, which becomes evident later on when the veneer wears off. He's deliberately not argumentative, always agrees with you to the point of absurdity and avoids disagreements altogether, as it is all part of the ruse to make him always 'look good'. It becomes cloying after a while, and you wonder if he can even think for himself, but there is a reason he does this.

Genuine nice guys will disagree and tell you why they are not happy with something because they are sincere in their relationships and do not just go along with everything you say and do. The Fake Mr Nice Guy, however, uses his 'niceness' as a way of first attracting then snaring you. That's when the truth comes out about him, and things begin to unravel. Then, you are the one with the problem because he is 'so nice'. He's a bit like an artificial sweetener – looks good, sounds great but has a nasty aftertaste.

CHAPTER 16

The Wife's Perspective and When 'It Hits the Fan'

Now that you have a clearer picture of why men have affairs, let's pause to consider things from the wife's perspective.

First rule of thumb: How do you know the married man you are seeing is lying to you? Follow your gut feeling and look for the signs that don't sync with what he tells you! Married men lie to their wives, to you and to themselves. He is a very good manipulator and knows just how to say what **he thinks you want to hear** (Read that bit again!) to get what he wants. As harsh as that is, we are dealing with a man who could be emotionally fractured in some way.

To gain your sympathy and trust, he tells you about his married life and how miserable he is but makes excuses about not being able to leave the marriage. He is such a martyr, and if awards were handed out for the rubbish he sprouts, he would be a proud recipient. So, what do you think he is saying to his wife?

Remember, he chose to marry her – you know, the whole 'To love and to cherish', 'To have and to hold', 'To forsake all others as long as you both shall live' bit. At the time, he meant it (or maybe he didn't). Now that he is bored, unhappy or whatever adjective he uses to describe his married life, his wife is doing her best.

Moving on a few years, both he and his wife will not be the same people as when they married. If his wife is as bad as he makes her out to be, then what happened between them to

a) turn her into a harpy, and

b) make him talk about her that way?

If she was always like that, do you think he would have married her? So, whatever he is bleating about, take it with a grain of salt because unless she has a mental illness, her character may not be anything like he is describing. (The most important red flag of all, so pay attention!)

She may not know about his indiscretions, but she looks after him, has children with him and looks after her family and the house as best she can, and she probably has a job on top of everything else. She is also intimate with him and loves him. So, how do you think she'll react when 'it hits the fan', and she finds out he is sleeping with another woman?

The Wife's Perspective and When 'It Hits the Fan'

From her perspective, what she will go through will be much worse than if he then cheated on you (not devaluing your feelings here). She is the one married to him; she built a life with him and, over the years, has nurtured and trusted him. If you stop and think about it, by cheating with you, he is also cheating on both of you. The difference is that you know about the 'Other Woman'.

I am not, by any means, trivialising the pain and emotional suffering either of you will feel when the truth emerges about the affair, but this is where you will see what he is truly made of. She will feel the emotions associated with betrayal more acutely. All the trust they shared – vows broken – and the man she knew for all those years deceived her. She is just as much a victim as you, and she will be shattered (and probably go supernova) when it all kicks off.

So, while he is cheating on his wife and badmouthing her, you are a willing accomplice to the cheating, mainly because of believing what he told you about his marriage. Of course, you would. He is such a great guy who deserves to be with someone better than what he has now – someone like you!

No judgements here; the facts speak for themselves. In his inability to connect with his wife about the problems in his marriage, two or more lives are now in the balance. Most certainly, life for you and his wife is going to change.

Have you ever heard the expression, 'Hell hath no fury like that of a woman scorned!'? Well, he is about to find out just what that will entail. If he thought his life was awful before she knew about his affair (and she will find out), then he has no idea how creative she will become when the story breaks. It doesn't matter what the situation between them is; the depth of how much she loved him is about to do a sharp 180 in the opposite direction.

His wife will be making big changes and doing some serious soul-searching in the days and weeks ahead as to her options (they both know she holds most of the cards), but her first thought will be for the children, if they have them. If she was in an abusive relationship, with him being the abuser, this **may** be her out, and you are welcome to him. (Be cautious if she lets him go so easily, as she may have good reason. Just sayin'!)

With the marital laws in place now in Australia, she stands to gain a minimum of half of everything they own together, but usually more if she has the kids (pre-nups notwithstanding). Moreover, if she has proof of his abuse, she can file charges. In that situation, it makes you think about whether she was as bad as he made her out to be and whether you want an abuser for a partner.

Likewise, if the abuse came from her, **he** then has to decide if living that life will damage him further and consider the positive steps he can take to protect himself and his kids from her. Either way, the abuse will all come out in the wash, and it will then be up to you to do what you feel is right for you. If you support him, your road ahead will be one of solidarity and healing. For him, it will be getting legal advice.

Another alternative is that the wife may decide to talk things through with him and then seek marital counselling. How invested he is in continuing the marriage will determine whether the counselling helps them stay together. At this stage, he may talk about his dissatisfaction and what led him to an affair.

The Wife's Perspective and When 'It Hits the Fan'

But no matter how long they are in therapy together, nothing will save that sinking ship if the rot has already set in.

If she is a vengeful person, then she will make sure he suffers. Anything from emailing everyone he knows, finding out who you are (as she is going to hold you responsible for this disaster) and worse – confronting you. Although innocent bystanders, the kids will be caught up in all this drama and can be used against him.

In short, his life is going to take on a roller coaster ride from hell, and that's even before divorce proceedings happen, if she even decides to go down that path. She may want to torment him as long as possible and refuse to divorce him. On the bright side, in Australia, the laws have changed in that you no longer need to have your spouse's permission or signature to get a divorce. You can even do it online, but there is a catch, as you'll both need to go to counselling (except under extenuating circumstance, like abuse, this may not happen). Once *divorce* is mentioned, however, he will have to consider just how much he will lose and whether you are the better option.

You will have to step up for your married man, if he hasn't already dumped you, which is certainly possible if she gives him an ultimatum. She has a lot of clout, and she knows it, so she will make life for you both as painful and difficult as she can to even the score.

Take inspiration from the song 'So What' by Pink

CHAPTER 17

Where Did It All Go Wrong for Him?

Because the married couple weren't able to communicate their frustrations regarding issues in their marriage, things between them began to deteriorate to the point of something drastic happening and breaking open that wound, which eventually led to him (or her) looking outside the marriage for relief and affection.

An affair primarily stems from the lack of communication between the couple and letting things slide. It would have been better to deal with the issues immediately rather than let them fester. The apathy and stifling routine boil down to not taking responsibility individually or as a couple, which impacts the relationship to collapse. Compounding that, if there is a lack of money and too many bills to pay, screaming kids, whining and arguing, other parties – like external family – interfering in the marriage and no end in sight for any of this to change, then the idea of marital bliss is idealistic nonsense.

The loss of intimacy is another nail in the coffin for the couple's marriage. How can you show love to someone who only expresses indifference towards you? An indifference progressively created and distorted over time to the point where week in, week out, year in, year out, nothing changes; it feels like you are serving a sentence for a non-existing crime. The frustration of wanting life to be different can be overwhelming. But because of either circumstance or refusal from the spouse to make changes, there is no going forward within the relationship.

He would feel totally out of his depth at what he is experiencing, yet all he can do is hang on. It is having to be responsible for providing everything the family needs and coping with the pressure of it all. When his kids were born, they would have been the best experience ever. But as they grew, the price of feeding, housing and schooling grew with them – not the child's fault, it's just how it is.

If he feels invisible watching how life is happening all around him, and it seems like he is not part of the world anymore – just a bystander helplessly watching from the sidelines – then not only is he not having his needs met but also depleting the reserves within him. That is when the fuse gets lit. (Enter the Other Woman!)

If he chooses to move out or confront his partner with his dissatisfaction about the marriage, it might trigger them to face the reality of their situation and their troubles head-on.

Where Did It All Go Wrong for Him?

Whether their relationship is worth salvaging will depend on how much they have been worn down over the years. If they both cannot continue as they had been, as things are not likely to change, they might want to call it quits and stop pretending to everyone that their marriage was OK when they both knew it wasn't. In that situation, no amount of talking, counselling or promises will mend the rot already set into their marital foundations. If they are honest with each other, then separating may not only be the best option but the healthiest one for all concerned, especially for the kids.

As hard as it is for children to cope with a family breakdown, it is just as damaging for them to be in a family where the parents are constantly at odds. That toxic environment will certainly affect them.

If the parents decide to remain together, they will have to up their game regarding the environment they provide for their children to grow up in. Yes, the children will play a large part in making the decisions needed for everyone's future. Still, they will only be one factor to consider and not necessarily the deal-breaker.

CHAPTER 18

An Affair Can Be the Best Thing for a Marriage

This is not what you want to read right now, but sometimes an affair brings everything to the surface and out from the shadows. When all has been said and done, and the light shines bright again for them, the marriage gets a clean slate and a fresh start, and the love between them may reignite. If they are committed to working things out by airing their differences, they begin to re-establish the basis for trust. So when any future problems arise, either one of them will be confident in feeling safe to discuss any issues and working on them.

Life does not come with a handbook of answers. It can be difficult navigating the journey or deciding the best course of action. Still, it always comes down to one simple fact: They both must take responsibility for themselves and what happens to them and their family. Simply put, 'If it is not right within you, then it will not be right outside of you either.'

When marriages fail and affairs start, it is because one or both people have not taken accountability – for themselves, their life and the decisions that need to be made. They ignore things when they happen or expect the other party to take on the obligation of fixing the problem because dealing with issues on top of everything else can be too much.

Apathy sets in, and they become stuck in misery unless one of them realises why their relationship is not working, takes that step forward and talks things through – provided the partner is willing to listen and work through the issues. If not, then their relationship will never progress. So, their lives, dreams, goals and growth become stagnant.

Instead of resolving the problems troubling them (their unhappy marriage), one person adds to it (by having an affair). So, not only is there a third party who is now tangled up in this Greek tragedy, but they are swept up in a drama entirely of that couple's making. However, when they both accept equal blame for the failure of their relationship, healing can come about. And if they are willing to work together to address issues, move forward and keep the problems between themselves, then the affair will have brought about constructive change for the couple.

Sometimes it takes a drastic measure, like having an affair, to clear the waters and force the couple to see where the damage is being done and, importantly, do something about it together.

We, as human beings, do the best we can with what we have. Life is hard; there are no set formulae for how to live your life, and we all muddle along, going from one experience to the next. Unless, of course, you're at a level of growth that allows you to operate from a higher perspective than the rest of the pack. Those who can look within themselves; recognise that the responsibility for their own happiness lies within; and not look externally for happiness, gratification, justification, worth and reason for existing are better able to cope with the road they travel through in life.

Just a note to contemplate

There is a lot to be said about reflection, open discussion, honesty, placing value on and liking yourself, knowing what not to accept from others, learning that true happiness starts within you and not relying on someone else to complete you. Yes, people will make you happy (externally), but they only complement the truth of your self-worth.

When you are out of your depth and your relationship is in trouble, seeking professional help may be the only option. Counsellors, psychologists, helplines and friends or family can be just who you need to talk to and make your way out of that misery to reach that quality of life you deserve.

CHAPTER 19

What About the Kids?

Much has been written about the impact on children when their parents separate and then divorce. No matter the child's age, if the parents have created a toxic home environment, there will be an existing foundation of stress and hostility from an unhappy home life. Adding a parent exiting the relationship, and the child's problems are compounded. However, there are times when a marriage breakup is the best thing for the child concerned. Most parents do not take into consideration just how damaging it is for the child to constantly hear the arguments and feel the hostility between the parents.

Despite the separation between parents, children will adjust to new situations as long as they are supported and their needs are met by both parents or carers, so their anxiety will be manageable. Yes, even children in nurturing environments can experience parents separating (It's all about their **parents'** troubles). Unfortunately, no one is immune from a marriage breakdown, but how children cope will depend on how much support and love they receive from their parents.

It is inevitable – when the parents have played a crucial role in shaping their children in one form or another – that the product of the parent's interaction determines the children's attitude and ability to deal with the family's breakup. When the decision becomes a reality and the parents split up, the die has already been cast regarding how the children respond and cope.

Even babies can understand the negative energy between people and will become unsettled and even distressed, reacting negatively to the hostility. Unhappy parents equate to an unhappy baby, which puts more pressure on the couple. The older the child becomes and remains in that toxic environment, the more detrimental the impact will be on their mental health as they grow.

The poem below sets out a perfect example of this:

Children Learn What They Live
by Dorothy Law Nolte

If a child lives with criticism, he learns to condemn.

If a child lives with hostility, he learns to fight.

If a child lives with ridicule, he learns to be shy.

If a child lives with shame, he learns to feel guilty.

What About the Kids?

If a child lives with tolerance, he learns to be patient.

If a child lives with encouragement, he learns confidence.

If a child lives with praise, he learns to appreciate.

If a child lives with fairness, he learns justice.

If a child lives with security, he learns to have faith.

If a child lives with approval, he learns to like himself.

If a child lives with acceptance and friendship, he learns to find love in the world.

If the parents are going to separate, it is important to talk with the child, at any age, and include them in what is happening every step of the way. Reassure them that they were not responsible for the breakup and that both parents love them. It is so important to explain how the parents' problems had nothing to do with the child.

The parents will be met with questions and tears, imploring them not to separate and probably a massive tantrum or many mini meltdowns, complete withdrawal, or change of character for a time. This is natural behaviour as they need time to process and come to terms with what is happening to the two most important people in their lives.

Once the parents split, and the child learns it is safe to be with both parents even if they are not together, they adjust. If their new family dynamic – with their mother's or father's new living arrangements – is positively reinforced by both parents, their developing behavioural issues will be kept to a minimum.

But here comes the curve ball. If 'abandoning' his children is such a major issue because he knows his wife's character and she could become vindictive, then he knows she may use the children as leverage in getting what she wants and how much he gets to see them. Prepare yourself because there will be a battle, and the children are stuck firmly in the middle.

Added to the mix are all the extended family on either side – think parents and grandparents, brothers and sisters, aunts, uncles, cousins and all their kids. Once news breaks that the relationship is over and one partner leaves, then families close ranks very quickly, especially when furnished with negative and caustic experiences by the member of their bloodline.

Another factor that comes into the equation is how the children will get along with you. Yes, there will be a transitional period of adjustment. But if both parents are supportive, give positive reinforcement, and the children see the positive change in their parents – plus you invest love and care in them – they will eventually respond well to the support and nurturing.

On the negative side, despite being old enough to understand their parents' unhappiness, the toxicity has already set in on older children, especially teens. No matter how much love and support they are given, they will justify their anger and bad behaviour by holding you responsible for breaking up their family. Their reasoning would be: Before you came along, they had a home and a mother and a father who all lived together. They were a family (toxicity between the parents aside). Now, you ruined everything (despite saving their father from a continued, unhappy existence), and they will not look kindly at anything you do for them.

Brutal fact, but you need to know what you are up against.

Your job is not to replace their mother but to be yourself and be there for them, which brings about its own challenges. They may need counselling, and it is important to talk about any issues or concerns you have regarding his children because communication is the key. But ultimately, the children's parents must work together to parent the children despite not being physically together. This does not mean you cannot have input in any decision, but your role is solely a supporting one.

CHAPTER 20

How Long Is This Going to Take?

Women are not rehabilitation centres for badly raised men.

It's not their job to fix him, change him parent or raise him.

You want a partner, not a project.

Julia Roberts

The longer you are with this married man, the longer you will end up feeling frustrated and dissatisfied with this relationship, increasingly feeling the urge to throttle him and then move on. You are stuck in a rut, and although you may still love him, you know that your gut is screaming at you, 'You're not happy!'

Is He Ever Going to Leave His Wife?

It's like watching and waiting for a kettle to boil – the longer you watch, the longer it takes. Same with your married man; the longer you wait for him doing nothing, happy to keep the current situation, the more you are confirming to him that even though you are not happy with this arrangement, you are prepared to wait for that miracle to happen, and one day you'll end up together.

WAKE UP! Yeah, he knows this. It is becoming a desperate situation. He has promised to leave his wife, but the days turn into weeks, which run into months and years. Before you know it, he has taken the best years of you (Selfish crud!). **But you are allowing this.**

Remind yourself how long you have been with him. How long have you listened to him sprout empty promises and then buy you something special to make up for not being able to leave? (Yes, he is that shameless!)

If you are true to yourself, you already know he is not leaving his wife despite what he says. No amount of cajoling, pleading, convincing or crying on your part will move him. (Heartless user beast!)

You love him, but the sad truth is that you are in love with being in love with him. There is a difference between the state of love and the idea of love – one is real, and the other is a fanciful hope. As hard as it will be, take a truthful assessment of why you have spent all this time waiting for him, afraid to let go:

- You don't want to be alone. (Do you know how many men there are in the world?)

How Long Is This Going to Take?

- You love him, and no one else can compare. (That may be a blessing, really! Thankfully, not all men are like him.)
- You have spent all this time with him, and it has come to nothing. (Honey, he is teaching you one of the most valuable lessons there is: how not to be treated.)
- If you leave him and he then leaves his wife, you may miss out on a future together. (So, he's waiting for you to leave him before he leaves his wife. Seriously? Read that bit again, aloud!)
- The thought of you not seeing him, being in contact with him or speaking to him is too much to bear. (It takes two weeks to break a habit – TWO WEEKS! So why cling to driftwood?)
- The pain of letting him go is too overwhelming for you.
- You're comfortable with your life with him, but you want to be with him so bad. (Being comfortable and living in constant hope has made you lose yourself, which you have done by not trusting your inner voice. You've got this!)

The truth is that your focus has always been primarily on him – his wants, needs, well-being, timeline, agenda – and he is the centre of your world. As a result, you have misplaced the person you once were because he has worn you down, and you no longer even know who you are. You have relinquished responsibility for yourself (Does he make all the decisions and call all the shots?), and everything that made you unique is all but gone. In short, you became someone else for him. Is it any wonder, then, you are having thoughts of abandoning ship?

Now you feel the way you do because you need to find yourself again. You need to get reacquainted with that beautiful woman who had so much life and dreamed about the things she could do and the places she would go. So how do you find yourself?

By not giving away your power to a man who does not deserve you. He already has the woman he deserves, and if she makes him happy or unhappy, then great! You deserve happy. We will talk more about reclaiming your power later. For now, this quote from Buddha sums up the reality you are living.

No one saves us but ourselves. No one can, and no one may. We ourselves must walk the path.
– Paul Carus, Karma: A Story of Buddhist Ethics

Just a thought and with analogy

Moving through life is like swinging from one vine to another, from one moment and situation to the next. But when you stop and keep holding on to the same vine, you become stuck, tired and eventually exhausted because you stopped the momentum by not letting go of that situation you are in. Unless you reach out for the next vine, you cannot move forward to catch the next adventure. So, let go of what is not serving you and look for that next vine.

CHAPTER 21

He Is Not Afraid to Lose You

*Some people's souls do not match their beautiful
faces, and that's why it is so crucial that you learn
how to read people's energy.*
Witches and Old Souls

As much as you trust that he will stay with you for the foreseeable future because your relationship is great (even though the situation is not ideal), he is holding all the cards. Not only does he know you love him and are true to him, but he knows you will remain faithful, unlike him – but that doesn't count because he's the man calling the shots.

With this relationship in play, not only is he getting the security of a home life away from you but also the bonus of living out his fantasy with you. So, what about your security? It's all great for him, while you and his wife are in separate compartments and towing your respective lines. But if you were to tip the scales suddenly and want more from the relationship, then he may not be agreeable to changing things between you.

Are you in any position to bargain with him, make demands or give him an ultimatum? If you think you are, then perhaps see what he is made of and how quickly he changes. He may not want to put up with someone who cannot keep her place, so unlike his wife, he **can** leave you (in a heartbeat). If life with you gets too uncomfortable in any way, then there are plenty of other women out there to fulfil his desires. (Conceited sod!)

He even has a plan in play if you decide to approach his wife. He will not only turn on you to side with her (Man, I've seen this happen, and it is not pretty!) – and get this – but he may even admit to the affair and make himself the victim because you seduced him (So, he doesn't know what the word *no* means?). Or, he will deny everything, and if he is cornered, he could even threaten you and question your sanity. That's how low this man is and how sure he is of himself; there are no lengths he will not go to when it comes to saving himself. Then, when the dust settles, he just picks up where he left off with someone else.

He knows the scales are tipped in his favour, so he's not at all worried about you bailing on him. As a matter of fact, he is so confident that you want him more than he does you that he plays you, knowing you are too insecure or innocent to see this. Please do not take this as a criticism of you. Your love for him is genuine, and he uses your kindness and goodness to his advantage. This is not love he has for you; he knows you are a convenient amusement, and he has a secure faith that you want him no matter the cost. (Megalomaniac creep!)

Yes, he says and does all the right things, treats you like his princess babe and keeps you just out of reach. So, you keep reaching for more, but you will inevitably wake up from his spell and see just how badly you have allowed him to treat you. This is not a failing in you because we all allow people to do this to an extent, so you will learn a valuable lesson from him about what not to put up with. (Yes, you do deserve better, and there is a special place in hell reserved for people like him!)

The emptiness and unfulfillment you feel are coupled with tinges of regret that you allowed this relationship to go on for as long as it did (Has it been over a year?). The sad thing is if you tell him it's over, you will not even get an argument from him after this long and will unlikely ask for an explanation, because he either doesn't care or is relieved he's not the one having to end things. He will just collect his gear and walk out. Transaction complete.

Well, if you are feeling the emptiness inside but are fearful of making the wrong decision, then don't be; your gut is telling you it's time to move forward with your life and wise up to him. But most of all, you need to learn to stop allowing him (or anybody) to treat you so badly.

You are worth so much more than what this man is giving you, so baby-steps away from him, and soon you will be strong enough to let him go. The section at the back of this book on how to get over him and the strategies to use will help you do what you need to reclaim yourself.

Is He Ever Going to Leave His Wife?

How do you know if he is not worried about losing you? If you are saying yes to any of the following, then know you are well and truly hooked with this guy and may need to evaluate your position.

- Are you the one endlessly waiting for him to leave his wife?
- You seem to always be anticipating his arrival to spend time with him.
- You love him, and he knows it, but your enthusiasm is waning.
- You do everything for him that his wife doesn't.
- You are the one he says he 'really' loves, but he hasn't proven it.
- He's told you there is this special connection between you, and while it tortures him to not be with you, he's still with his wife.
- You are bending over backwards to accommodate him in whatever he wants.
- The scales are always tipped in his favour.
- You need to fit into his timeline.
- You make contact more than he does.
- He only calls you from where he works or on his mobile.
- He doesn't like his photo being taken.
- You have been with him for more than a year.
- You feel time is against you, and your body clock is ticking LOUDLY!
- You are fearful of leaving him because thoughts of being alone unsettle you.
- You are disagreeing with each other more.
- You feel increasingly frustrated.
- You begin to have pangs of anger about him and this relationship.

He Is Not Afraid to Lose You

- You always back down in a disagreement (or now, maybe you don't!).
- You are questioning why you are even with him.
- You begin to see his true nature and how he plays you.
- You feel trapped with him.
- You begin to resent the power he has over you.
- You are disappointed with your life.
- You realise you are worth better than the crumbs he is giving you. (Hell Yeah!)
- He's no longer the person he was when you first got together.
- You are with him out of habit.
- You are revisiting thoughts of removing his bits!

CHAPTER 22

Dumped by a Married Man

There is nothing so emotionally painful than when a relationship is over, and you now must cope with the fallout and pick up the pieces of the wreckage he left you with. The heartbreak you suffer and the emotions you need to contend with – like confusion, sadness, shame, guilt, anger and regret – are brutal, even though they may not all be justified. You will also need emotional help.

If he made the decision to call it quits and up and left, thank your lucky stars he did – despite how your relationship ended. You will soon come to the realisation that you are not a piece of rubbish to be discarded. However, at present, you are feeling the emotions so intensely because of how much you loved him and how easily he let you go. (Man, is he in for some heavy-duty KARMA, BABY!)

Is He Ever Going to Leave His Wife?

There are two important issues affecting you right now. First is how to deal with the pain you are going through. Second, you want answers as to **why** it happened.

Dealing with the pain of a breakup is excruciating, and it is as real as a physical blow. The degree of how much you will react to having the rug pulled out from under you will depend on whether the breakup was a gradual progression until the axe fell or it came out of the blue.

So, let's deal with the *why* factor first.

IT WAS NOT YOUR FAULT, AND YOU HAVE NO BLAME IN WHAT HAPPENED. YOU ARE NOT A LESSER PERSON BECAUSE OF THE EXPERIENCE, SO BE GENTLE AND KIND TO YOURSELF, OK?

Read that again!

So, get those depressive and inaccurate thoughts about yourself out of your head. Despite what you might think, they are unsubstantiated and wrong. Every woman I have spoken to has felt like that, so trust the process and take one moment at a time for now.

Despite having seen or felt the signs of the breakup looming, you ignored that feeling within you. When the end finally happened (Amazing how he was able to summon up the courage to leave you but not his wife. What does that tell you?), you were floored. Perhaps you did not think it would come about because you believed you loved each other. He told you as much, often, and he kept saying how unhappy he was with his wife. So, why did he break up with you and not her?

If he just announced it was over (Did he even have the decency to let you know in person, or did he just text you?) without a feasible explanation, it was not only cruel of him to end things that way, but it also shows his lack of compassion and integrity. (There are a few choice words we can call him right now, but we are better than that.)

The most plausible reason for the abrupt end was that his wife found out about you and gave him an ultimatum (An ultimatum always works when the wife gives it to her husband but rarely does it work when a lover gives the same). This would explain his sudden departure and his not explaining anything to you.

Or, perhaps, he was bored and wanted excitement from a new woman (Remember the vine analogy where you let go of one vine after you have grabbed onto the other? Well, maybe that's what he has just done.). He has found someone else, and you are now surplus to needs. BUT THIS IS A GOOD THING! If he treats you like this, be grateful you are now free of him to start healing, make yourself a priority, and be with someone a whole, hell-of-a-lot better than him.

You may think that me saying, 'This is a good thing' is the biggest load of bull dinky, but he has just thrown you under the bus and revealed the type of man he really is. (Therefore, he did you a favour. Win-win, honey!)

Do not, for even a millisecond, think you do not deserve better from anyone else because you love him so much (Yes, women have actually said this to me!). Look at what he has done to you – how he has eroded your confidence and self-worth, so you increasingly settle for less. Well, I am giving you the permission you will not give yourself to re-evaluate your

Is He Ever Going to Leave His Wife?

beautiful self and get to know that person you have lost – the one you see looking back in the mirror.

You may be fractured now, but you are not completely broken. We will work on that. Even if you do not believe you have a right to a much better life, I am here to tell you that it really does start with you. You may not feel or think that way at present, but one day you will be fully free of him and be in a better, stronger place – emotionally and mentally. And, damn, girl, you are going to shine.

His decision to let you go has nothing to do with you, even though you try and justify that reasoning to make sense of the *why*. This whole affair has always been about him. If you understand this fact, you can better cope with moving forward and not internalise his motive. If you feel and think you had done something wrong, well, you didn't. The only thing you did was love him and give him what he needed. (Unless you had done something wrong, like telling his wife about you – naughty. But roll with it now!)

Perhaps you think this is the thanks you get for everything you did for him (Well, he is a selfish, thankless beast!). No wonder you are feeling all these emotions surge through you. He is the coward in all this, while you are the better person because you are still here, integrity intact, still standing and carrying on for another day. You may feel shattered, but you are not finished with yourself yet, and the best is yet to come!

Now that you understand the dynamics of the breakup a little better, dealing with the significant effect on your emotions, mental health and physical well-being is the key to getting over him.

Important

If you think you are likely to have a breakdown, and your mental health has suffered because of the ordeal you have just been through, then perhaps getting further help from a professional is what you need. They are equipped to deal with the trauma of these mental issues and give you sound strategies to regain your mental health.

Do not hesitate to call and make an appointment with a professional counsellor or psychologist, or phone a helpline or a doctor, as they can help you when you most need it. There is no shame in asking for help, especially after this situation. You have suffered trauma and need care and compassion right now.

Take inspiration from the song
'Someone You Loved' by Lewis Capaldi

CHAPTER 23

How to Stop Being Obsessed With a Married Man

He is everywhere – in your head, the songs you listen to, the places you used to visit, the things he gave you – all reminders of what used to be and now no longer. You just cannot seem to get him out of your head, and he is in every fibre of your being. All you want is to not be up at three in the morning, crying.

Even though you will vacillate between wanting and repelling him, the pain you are going through is powerful. He has affected you immensely, and the pendulum has swung to its full arc both ways. First, in such a fantastic positive way when you were deliriously happy together. Now when the pendulum has reached the opposite apex, the cruelty of abandonment and all the negative aspects you are experiencing have hit you with the force of a 747 jet. Man, that sux!

Even though his essence will linger and remain with you for some time (a bit like a spell that won't be broken), his energy will haunt your thoughts until you can deal with that. There will be moments, out of nowhere, when you can smell his cologne, hear his laugh in a crowd or see someone that looks like him, and the thoughts and feelings start up again. So, you need a little magic of your own to banish his ghost.

Let's evict this troublesome tenant from your mind and let you get a good night's sleep. But how do you get over someone you love so much and stop thinking about them? The simple answer is: gently.

The longer you have been with him or the more intense the relationship was, even if it was for a short time, the more of an impact he has had on you. So, you will have to take decisive action gently and calmly for yourself.

If you can first understand the *how*, while you cannot help whom you fall in love with (or maybe you can!), you can consciously help yourself to un-love them again. There is always a good reason why things happen the way they do, even if we do not know what that reason is until much later. This may help you take some of the load off your mind.

Despite how much you have invested in him, you now need to invest that same energy in yourself. Take that equivalent love and commitment you gave him and give that to yourself. The more you work on yourself, the quicker you will get over him and break free of his hold on you. In addition, because you begin to invest in doing right by yourself, this will give you the strength to 'recall your power back from him' (more on this later). But the very first thing you do is look yourself in the mirror and say out loud:

'I AM WORTH EVERYTHING I DO FOR MYSELF. I AM NOT GOING TO LET HIM TAKE ANY MORE FROM ME, AND HE NO LONGER HAS ANY POWER OVER ME!'

> Look in the mirror and say that aloud to yourself a few times each morning. Or, each time you begin to think about him, say, 'YOU NO LONGER HAVE ANY POWER OVER ME.' The more you say it, the more you ingrain that in yourself. Therefore, your energy, thoughts, feelings and emotions will begin to change and ground you to heal you.

Yes, this may sound a little out there, but the way you think has a lot to do with what you believe. The more positive you are in your thoughts, the more the world around you will shift to the positive. As Robert, my Tai Chi instructor, simply puts it, 'If you think you can, or you think you can't, you are dead right!' Powerful stuff when you get the concept and apply it.

Any time you actively think about what went wrong, where things broke down, and how you could have done things differently, **just stop.** Take a breath (say the above line) and stop torturing yourself about why he chose her over you. If you understand it was not a competition between you and his wife because you were never in the running, as he chose to stay married to her, then quite frankly, she is welcome to him!

Stop any scenario with an 'If only' attached to it. These are minefields you walk through, trying to justify the *why* of something. You cannot change the past. It does not matter how much you reinvent a scenario in your head to try for a different outcome or wish, hope, pray or try and will him to come back. Once that page has turned, don't look back. Ultimately, it will always end up the same because it was your journey, no matter how much you feel otherwise. So, stop torturing yourself over a jerk who didn't deserve you.

If you catch yourself thinking about him, say out loud or whisper, 'You have no power over me. I take back my power!' By saying these words every time you begin thinking about him, his power over you will lessen. It sounds a little trippy, but it works. By saying it out loud, energetically and to the universe – especially to him – you break the energy connection he still holds you with.

The power of the mind is phenomenal, and to reinforce your desire to rid him from your life and your mind, the simple act of reclaiming your power does just that. Before you know it, his strength and hold over you diminishes as your mind and mental health become stronger. So, trust this process and say those words with conviction. You're an awesome woman. You've got this!

A word of warning

You will go through the grief of losing that relationship. On that note, if you get stuck at the angry stage, eliminate any thoughts of brewing revenge. Not only is revenge reacting to his bad behaviour with equally bad behaviour, but things can get ugly and out of control really fast. What may be a few moments of supposed payback to even up the scales may turn into a nightmare (I've seen it happen – police, court, the works). So, step away and take a breath.

---

*Take inspiration from the song
'Release Me' by Agnes*

CHAPTER 24

What Not to Do

You are at that point in disbelief where your life had been floating along without too much turbulence. Whether the relationship eroded over time or you were blindsided, it is understandable how you feel is like having been in a car crash.

The emotions surging within you, if it were an electric current, could run a small city! Man, that was rough, and all you can think about is taking that sucker out. OK, breathe. As much as you are devastated (undeservedly so, may I add), any thoughts of revenge are going to be counterproductive because you are better than that (Yes, you are!), and revenge will hurt you more than it does him.

Even if you don't give a flying fig what happens to him now, **you** need to pick yourself up by the bootstraps and move forward without any comeback on you. Thoughts of all the terrible things you could do to him and certain parts of his anatomy all look great in your head, but nothing good ever comes from wanting to kill or maim the dude.

Firstly, none of this was about you. As much as you scrutinise every little scenario in your head and replay the whole affair for clues as to where you may have gone wrong, for the sake of your sanity, IT WAS NOT YOU!

OK, if on the unlikely chance that it was you:

a) It was all meant to be, so just roll with it.
b) Him ditching you is a good thing because it means he was not interested in fixing things and making it work with you.
c) He does not have the internal fortitude to do what it takes to be with you, regardless of what happened. He is a coward to boot!
d) He probably drove you to do whatever you did, anyway.

OK, here are the things you must not do despite how tempting the idea is:

1: DO NOT, under any circumstance, contact his wife and tell her about your affair.

This must come from him. You may think it is a good idea to let her know about what you have both been up to, hoping she will kick him out or he will be forced to leave her and return to you. This ambush will not go well for you and may very likely backfire big time (Seen that happen too many times not to trust this.). It never **ever** goes the way you think it will, so don't go there.

2: DO NOT deliberately become pregnant.

This will fall under the 'Hell No' category. If you are still with him and think that by getting pregnant you force the situation so he leaves his wife, think again. You are seriously ambushing him with this course. Unless you have discussed this with him, and he agrees to leave his wife because he wants to have children but his wife is unable to (Has he been tested for firing blanks?), this type of surprise will cause you both a whole world of hurt.

The repercussions of bringing his child into the world will affect the child as much as both of you. There is no reason whatsoever that this is a good idea. So, as much as you love him, this will not be the way to his heart.

3: DO NOT do anything illegal.

This means anything that will make him call the police or take a restraining order out on you. He is a cur for doing what he did to you and his wife, but don't let his bad behaviour result in you being punished. Anything you think you can do to him in retaliation will have consequences that will stay with you, like a police record (good luck keeping that from an employer). So, take hold of those thoughts and perhaps write them down in detail instead. Then delete them. Don't send them to him because it will be evidence against you if he needs to go there.

Firstly, you will be the one looking unhinged, especially if it comes out of the blue and he knows who is responsible for the misdeed (like keying his car or throwing a brick through the lounge window – and no, these are not suggestions to take up!). There are so many cameras around, you will likely be filmed at the time. So, leave him and his property well alone because, aside from your broken heart, you do not need to deal with an arrest as well.

While we are talking criminal intent, it's a bad idea to go hire a hitman! They are expensive and unreliable and will snitch on you in a pinch. Leave that to his wife to take him out.

Furthermore, you do not know how he will react and what he will do to you if he is cornered by having to explain why he needs to take police action. People are unpredictable when placed in a position where they need to defend themselves against an attack. While you may think you know him, you will not be prepared for what he is capable of.

4: DO NOT internet revenge post.

Social media can be one of the most damaging platforms for sharing news and shaming someone. It may feel like justice is being done at the time, but nothing is ever gained from being a troll on social media. It will give the victim ammunition about your state of mind, even though it may be justified because of the way you were treated. But you do not want to make your situation worse by posting bad things about him. If you need to vent, then do so personally – not in a public arena.

What Not to Do

So, here's the recommendation.

In your case, the **only** thing to do is delete everything there was between you (this eliminates any remnants of his bad energy) and then block him everywhere: Facebook, Instagram, Snapchat, WhatsApp or wherever you both connected. Truly! I know you don't want to do this because you still have strong feelings for him and think that if you delete his texts and photos, then you will have nothing left of him, meaning things between you are seriously over.

Hanging onto anything only reinforces how much you make these reminders 'precious'. Not a good thing! By hanging onto his photos, texts, whatever – thinking this will help you ease the pain as you eventually get over him – will only prolong the suffering. If he was worth hanging onto, he would be with you now and not withdrawn from your life.

Furthermore, these texts and the like are harmful for another reason, especially if they are explicit. One woman I spoke to found the wife's profile and sent everything she and the husband had exchanged. This was a man the Other Woman loved fiercely, yet he became unrecognisable in his rage and sought his own revenge, which nearly killed her.

There is nothing you need to keep of his that puts a dagger in your heart, which reminds you of what you **had** together. When you are stronger, say goodbye on your terms.

As a side note: As much as you may not believe in karma, let me tell you that no one has ever done wrong to someone and got away with it. Sooner or later, they will have to pay for their sins, so concentrate 100% on yourself because the best revenge – and what will really stick the knife in – is for you to be truly happy without him. As they say, 'The best revenge is a fabulous life.' So you go, gorgeous girl!

xxx

CHAPTER 25

Going Through the Grief

God removes certain people from your life ...

Because he hears conversations you don't.

The sadness and pain you are feeling are normal responses when you are going through the stages of grief. Depending on the closeness to the person or the gravity of the relationship you had, you may go through the full seven stages of Denial, Anger, Bargaining, Depression, Acceptance, Guilt and Numbness, but not necessarily in the order stated.

With any loss – whether it is the loss of a family member, friend, love of your life, job or even a family pet – you will go through a period where you will feel the absence and transition to recovery. There will be times when, perhaps, you experience a relapse and go through a particular stage more than once – anger is certainly a candidate for repetition. If that is the case, accept that this is all part of the healing process and go with it.

So, what are the stages of grief?

The stages of grief, while they apply to any loss and varying degrees[12], can manifest differently for each person.[13] We will all react differently, depending on many factors that stem from our beliefs and circumstance to the level of faith we have to cope with the loss.

Below is a summary of what you may experience:

Denial

Denial is the first stage; whether consciously or subconsciously, this is the stage where you go into a state of shock. It is almost like the mind is preparing you for the sadness to come and the reality of the loss. It is a coping strategy to give you the time and the breathing space to acknowledge the loss.

Anger

This emotion is closely associated with the helplessness of being unable to prevent the loss. The anger can be directed either towards the person you have lost, thinking about why they have left you or towards yourself.

Bargaining

Human beings are a logical species. We need to understand why something has happened, which gives us peace in knowing the reason.

In this bargaining phase, you reason with the higher power to take the pain away, cope with the loss or help you understand why it happened. You may also find yourself exchanging something within you to take the pain away. Like, 'I promise never to get involved with a married man again. Just please take this pain away.'

Depression

While depression is part of the grieving process, it is at this stage that you spiral downwards. Symptoms may include extreme sadness – perhaps even loss of appetite and insomnia. This is because the mind continues to work overtime in accepting what happened, what the future holds and how you are affected by this loss.

Acceptance

Time really does heal all wounds. At this acceptance stage, the passage now focuses on you who has been grieving rather than on the married man you lost. At this stage, there is the acceptance of living without that person. As one day turns into the next, coping becomes easier as the wounds heal.

Guilt

This stage can happen any time throughout the seven stages because guilt will have you face the reality of that situation. It is one of the most confronting stages and one where you will be truthful with yourself. The upside to guilt is that you begin to take responsibility for yourself and own your part in things without blame, but this stage is also a very powerful teacher.

Guilt is inevitable, but once you work through the healing process and begin to involve yourself in activities, the healing process overpowers the feelings of guilt. At this stage of grief, when you become stronger, guilt will subside.

Numbness

At some stage, you will feel numbness when expecting emotions to wash over you. Some people just hit a wall, unable to feel anything. No sadness, no anger, no denial – nothing.

This may come early in the loss when you go into shock at the departure. You will either stay at this stage for some time, as it might take a while to absorb and comprehend what has happened or bounce from numbness to anger before progressing onto another stage. However, it is perfectly normal to feel nothing at all. It is the mind's way of protecting you from the reality of loss until you are better able to cope.

More on coping

To best cope with loss, you can try writing your feelings and expressing what you are going through. Writing helps you come to terms with your emotions and lessens the burden your mind is undertaking when dealing with what is happening to you.

Physical activity also plays a huge part in relieving the symptoms of grief. It not only helps you physically focus on the activity – like walking, jogging, cycling, gym work or even yoga – but the activity also helps with lowering stress levels. As you exercise, the brain releases endorphins, calming you and aiding in your healing. If you are unsure as to the suitability of exercise you want to undertake, seek a consultation with your doctor.

Important Note

If the grief lingers for more than a few months at most, consider speaking to your doctor or a professional counsellor about the loss. They are equipped to help you with coping strategies, and the sessions are strictly confidential. You will feel much better talking with a professional than with one of your friends, as a counsellor is trained in what you are going through. Your friends will always have your best interest at heart and have your back, but when it comes to grieving over a married man, they may not be as supportive or sympathetic.

If you feel your grief is affecting your life, work, enjoyment of activities and social interaction, then maybe you need to seek the help of a medical practitioner, counsellor or reach out

Is He Ever Going to Leave His Wife?

to Lifeline and speak to someone about what you are going through. You can also look up the Beyond Blue website[14], which has excellent pages on loss and coping with grief.

CHAPTER 26

How to Heal From This

We are all vulnerable and reactionary to the harshness of what the world can throw at us. Now, our ability to recognise what is happening 'within us' enables us to then deal with the issue and overcome the pain.

In his inspirational videos on YouTube and Instagram, Aaron Doughty coined the phrase, 'If you don't feel, you don't heal.'[15] Read that bit again because that is powerful stuff.

He describes how we first need to recognise why we are not healing from the pain and cannot move on from someone. We attach importance to them, which manifests within us. The more we hold onto that thought process – always thinking about them, wanting answers and a resolution – the more difficult it will be to let them go. It is a paradox.

Is He Ever Going to Leave His Wife?

You must feel and acknowledge the emotions you are experiencing from the loss and grief in order to heal from them. Don't be afraid of feeling sadness, heartache, pain or other negativity within you. Instead, you must walk through those shadows and allow yourself the time and space to truly feel to heal. Immerse yourself in this emotion, not fear it.

The fear comes from thinking that once you allow yourself to feel the pain, that will be all you feel from then on. It is an Attachment Hunger[16] we learn as babies and young children. When we see our mothers leave us alone in a room, we think we'll never see them again. But in fact, she has just nipped out to another room for a minute. Our reaction to this scary thought is to begin screaming.

That attachment loss is the same principle we feel in adulthood, bringing forth all the fear and elements of grief. Therefore, you do not want to face any negative emotion, and you either block it out or ignore it so as not to deal with it. That emotion then becomes part of us. We look at the situation through a lens distorted with unhealed emotions.

So, to deal with healing, it is vital to allow yourself to bring those painful emotions to light and feel everything brought up by experiencing that pain. I know you are repelling the idea here, trying to get away from having to deal with this. Still, it is necessary and a very sound way to get over and heal those negative feelings within you.

A few things to try:

Try setting yourself a goal, as that does wonders in moving you forward. It could be as simple as going on that holiday you have always dreamed of or setting yourself another target. What's important is to look to the future and have something to strive for. Being stuck and not knowing what to do with yourself can be defeating, and you will stay longer in the rut.

Be true to what you feel and allow yourself to deal with it any way you see fit to get over and eliminate that from within you (except going over to where he lives and spray painting the garage door – again, not a suggestion!). It may be screaming at the top of your lungs into your pillow (don't forget the pillow) and crying until you run out of tears. Or, if meditating, writing, speaking with a professional counsellor or perhaps keeping a journal of your feelings is your thing, then do whatever works for you.

The exercise is to evict your body's negative emotions, allowing you to come to terms with what you have just endured. Think of it as walking through a short, dark tunnel with the exit brightly showing you the way. You may walk through the darkness, but the light gets bigger as you get closer until you are emersed into the brightness and have left that darkness behind.

Treat this experience like ripping that Bandaid off the wound. You know it will hurt when you rip the thing off, but only for a short time because you allow the fresh air and light to heal the wound. That is what you will be doing to your mental health and well-being.

Take inspiration from the song 'Try' by Pink

CHAPTER 27

What If He Wants to Come Back?

You are just getting back on your feet, and out of the blue, he turns up at your door. You look sensational because you have been looking after and working on yourself. You are much stronger mentally – and immediately remember how you have been treated and burned by this man.

After your heart recovers from the massive jolt of seeing him in person again, you cling to the doorframe and ask him what he wants.

(Wait for it …)

He tells you how sorry he is for treating you so badly.

Is He Ever Going to Leave His Wife?

(His choice, not yours.)

Then, he goes on about how his wife is worse than ever.

(Well, can you blame her? If this is how you treat women, then your nuts should be in a vice, buddy!)

That you look fantastic and so sexy (and you see that familiar glint in his eyes).

(You raise one eyebrow in a 'Well, what did you expect? You broke me, and I did some mending.' kind of way)

That he can't live without you.

(Well, TRY! You had to learn to do that, so can he!)

And he wants to make it up to you.

(This is where you slam the door in his face.)

Is he delusional? Please don't say you are thinking about taking him back. But if you are having a moment of total insanity, then you must be tough as nails from now on. No more of this doormat behaviour because that simply isn't you anymore. Treat him mean to keep him keen!

He had demolished you once; remember what it took for you to claw your way out of that abyss. All the work you have done on yourself was well worth it, and you began to come out the other side of that darkness. In fact, he has taught you that 'a great life is nothing less than you deserve'.

What If He Wants to Come Back?

Don't forget he was not afraid of losing you when he cheated with you on his wife; that's why he let you go so quickly. So what's to say he won't cheat on you too or do the same thing to you again? Once a snake, always a snake; he just sheds his skin to grow bigger – or has he really learned his lesson?

If you do decide to give 'Nuts in a Vice' another chance, then it will be you calling the shots. If he's not happy with that arrangement, he is welcome to walk back out the door and back to his life.

Be very clear here: If you do take him back, make sure you are not deceiving yourself that it will be all bliss and roses again. If you find yourself rationalising why you are taking him back and trying to convince yourself he has changed, then stop and take a breath.

The first thing he must do to prove himself is to leave the family home. If he starts with excuses about not being able to leave her, then all he really wants is to use you again. NOPE, SORRY! Been there; not going there again. You are not someone he comes to when he needs to dump his problems. You are not his counsellor, his good time when he gets bored and certainly not just a body to have sex with.

HELL NO! It is going to be your way or the highway with this man.

He needs to understand that you have grown from that ordeal and will not tolerate bad behaviour like before. If he wants you back, he has to work super hard to win you over to prove that he is genuine this time. The strategies I wrote about in Chapter 10 will go a long way in helping you achieve the right result for you.

Is He Ever Going to Leave His Wife?

The bottom line is that unless he is prepared to change his circumstances without excuses and be true to you without delay (unless you are a glutton for punishment), he doesn't deserve five minutes of your time, so cut that loser loose.

---

*Take inspiration from the song
'Cry Me a River' by Justin Timberlake*

CHAPTER 28

The Stigma of Being the Other Woman

As if life wasn't hard enough, when you announce to your friends that you are in love with a man you met recently, they would naturally be thrilled for you and want to know all the details – all of them! The moment you tell them, 'Oh, he's married', watch how their reactions change. A moment ago, they were your best buds; they would take a bullet for you, and they are your sisters-from-other-misters!

'What, are you insane?' they say, almost choking on their bubbly. 'Why are you seeing a married man? This is a bad move, babe. Nothing but heartbreak will come from it.'

Then, they order more bubbly and begin to have a serious talk with you about the perils you are facing with a Married

Man. Incidentally, this is where you will separate the wheat from the chaff, as some of your friends will not want anything more to do with you.

Their reaction comes from age-old core beliefs and social standing – whether religious or cultural in origins – that date back to biblical times. For example, a woman considered to have loose morals and was paid for her services was cast out from society and thus was forced to be homeless and walk the streets. The **scarlet woman** has its origins from the book of Revelation in the Bible, referring to a prostitute. However, over time, the term also included women who have affairs with married men.

Society is entrenched in the principle that marriage is the most sacred undertaking two people will participate in to consolidate their commitment to each other. So, is it any wonder that in religious marriage ceremonies, the person marrying them says, '… and forsaking all others as long as you both shall live' during the couple's vows to each other (before God and all those here present)? To seal the deal, and so there is no misunderstanding, the Officiant announces to everyone that this couple is exclusive by adding '… let no man (or woman) put a sunder.'

And if history and the Oxford Dictionary remain to be believed, then you, as a woman having an affair with a married man, are his mistress; a home wrecker; a kept woman and his bit of skirt; his bit-on-the-side; a doxy (archaic); concubine (lower-ranking wife or lover); a courtesan (Italian); lover; the fancy woman or ladylove; if you are educated, then you are a hetaera (Greek); an inamorata (Italian); and if you must, his 'main squeeze'. They get worse from there, except not in any terms you would find in a dictionary, as they are colloquial slang.

The Stigma of Being the Other Woman

The Oxford Dictionary describes a *mistress* as a woman (other than the man's wife) having a sexual relationship with a married man.[17] Meanwhile, *stigma* means a mark of disgrace associated with a particular circumstance, quality or person. (Oh, please. Really?)

OK, enough name-calling. We get the gist! Did anyone ever consider the woman's position in this? Why is she always the one scorned and not the man? Is it because it really is a man's world? Men tend to get away with all sorts of bad behaviour when it comes to things like affairs, but the woman is always the one whom suspicion and scorn fall on, whether deserved or not.

Interestingly, when I looked up the word *mistress*, as we have just observed, there is a glut of definitions (some names less savoury than others). But for a man in the same position, astonishingly, there are just a few! There is a *manstress* (Is that a thing?), a *paramour* (very French) – although, it can be used for either man or woman but has the same implication – and a *gigolo* (but he tends to be young and gorgeous and worth every cent!).

History and English lessons aside, women get a bad rap. But, especially because it takes two people to make a relationship, and as the married man is half of the relationship, he is also half to blame in the affair. Yet, unbelievably, this fact remains somehow overlooked. You never hear of a single man getting ridiculed or having to live down being party to a relationship with a married woman. Instead, these men are envied and even patted on the back by their friends for accomplishing this achievement – 'The lucky dog', his friends say! (Gods give me strength – Neanderthals!)

Is He Ever Going to Leave His Wife?

All that aside, the way to deal with this unrealistic, unfair and unwarranted stigma is to ignore it. People will think whatever they like, and if their judgement of you is based on long-held beliefs on social morals, then there is little you can do about it but walk away. People will judge you whether they know you or not, and they will do so according to their viewpoint (and your care factor on their opinions needs to be set at zero!).

Your **true** friends will stick with you through thick and thin. They may disapprove of what you are doing only because they care enough about you and don't want to see you hurt when he can't leave his wife. Still, they have your back and want you to remain happy. They are the people you keep in your life whom you will need for support when life takes an unexpected turn in whatever direction. They will rejoice when he leaves his wife and you end up together, or they will be right there to pick up the pieces of your life with you because they are your real friends.

In an interesting article in YourTango, Tom Miller describes three categories[18] of Other Women, and he doesn't hold back when he describes each – I've tempered it a little (OK, brace yourself):

Mistress

More permanent in relationship, similar to that of his wife, and both women know about each other.

The Stigma of Being the Other Woman

Side Chick

Has less status than the mistress because she generally does not know he is married, but all his friends know about his side chick.

Jump-Off

These are not exclusive – perhaps sporadic in meeting – but purely for sex when they text at odd hours to see if they want an immediate hook-up.

Stigma turns to insults in the blink of an eye.

CHAPTER 29

Why Am I Always Attracting Married Men?

You meet him, and there is an instant attraction. Soon your feelings for each other spiral out of control. Straight for the hotel room, then?

You start seeing more of him, and he is just 'Wow!'. At some point, however, either you ask him or he tells you he is married. Not again? (No bother rushing off to the nearest mirror to check if there is a tattoo on your forehead saying, 'Only Married Men Need Apply'.)

Are there any available men left in the world? Are all married men cheating troglodytes? Well, yes and no. There are plenty of available men who are looking for a single lady they can love and cherish. Just keep sending out the single man vibes, honey, and no, thankfully, not all married men are maladjusted disasters, but the married ones you meet are the ones who go prowling for their next victim on places like dating sites where they have easy access to available women. (Lecherous beasts!)

Some women seem to repeat the same issue over and again. If you are one of these women who seems to always land a married man, then you may be unintentionally triggering his **hero instinct**[19], which men seem to love in a woman.

Men love being the hero, saving women from anything that might 'harm the damsel in distress'. They love being the man of the hour and the one who saves the day. He is a man, and that's what men do – protect the weaker sex (uh-huh!). If he is not getting that hero instinct triggered by his wife, another lady might. This all happens subconsciously in him and maybe with the woman who triggers this in him.

You may be just his type, and if you give him the vulnerable vibe, he will step up. In his online book, His Secret Obsession, James Bauer goes into the intricacies of this phenomenon. It makes sense, really, when you think males have always been bigger, stronger and more able to defend their clan or group. Even from the days of early human interactions, this instinct had already developed.

Now in modern-day relationships, there is no need to fight off sabre tooth tigers – or other cavemen – to protect their women (Well, they may still have to fight off an ape or two at clubs and rave parties). So, if you trigger this hero instinct unconsciously or otherwise, chances are you have pushed all the right buttons within him.

Why Am I Always Attracting Married Men?

The obvious thing to do, of course, is to jokingly ask this lovely man when he asks you out, 'Are you single or attached in some way?' Then, see what he says. If he is legitimate, he will tell you straight that he is not attached. But if he either begins telling you a sob story about his relationship or just laughs and doesn't say anything, you will know he has something to hide.

While this is an innocent and non-intrusive way to find out about him, it will be up to him to tell you the truth. So, watch his body language. He will send off clues as to whether he is lying or not. For example, look at his eyes; if he is lying, he will break eye contact and his eyes may dart about. Don't ignore this, as he may be lying, so do some more digging. 'So, you are single, right?'

A good book about body language is Body Language: How to Read Others' Thoughts by Their Gestures, written by Allan Pease.[20] He gives you a good framework on which to draw on. You can also simply look up *body language* on the internet, as there are lots of articles or books on the subject. It is important you learn a little about reading people, as this will save you from future heartbreak if you want to know if the man you met is lying about being married.

The dating scene is very complicated and sometimes perilous. It is unfair a married man who doesn't want to leave his marriage puts himself out there, not caring who he eventually hurts. What's worse is that while his actions may be reprehensible, they are not illegal. So, the best thing you can do for yourself is to be a little more attentive to what vibe you are getting from him, what your gut is telling you, and what his body language is saying when you ask him about his marital status.

Is He Ever Going to Leave His Wife?

You **will** find that handsome, genuine, fun-to-be-with man who is single and free to love you for the beautiful person you are. So, keep asking questions and trust yourself.

CHAPTER 30

The Office Romance Gone Bad

Ever wonder why there is a sound but logical workplace rule about not fraternising with those you work with? It is because the powers that be know that two people working together need to keep things professional and not get tangled up with each other. It is bad for the parties involved and bad for business.

Anywhere there are men and women working together for the same company, organisation, force or body, you can bet there will be rules against romance or intimate relations between colleagues. And you probably know why: If relationships between these colleagues stray beyond the boardroom and into the bedroom, then crossing those boundaries will not end well for them or the company.

Is He Ever Going to Leave His Wife?

Yes, the temptation to submit to your feelings for each other may be irresistible (and who will know if you are both discreet?). But think about the consequences this romance will have if it ends.

At work, you are professional and efficient, you are great at your job, and you really love what you do. However, there is this person working for the company (or who owns it), who you just cannot stop seeing – and he is married. (Double whammy!)

Everything is going great until it isn't. When an office relationship fails, it fails spectacularly, and you are completely exposed in the workplace. You need to have very thick skin (like the hide of a crocodile) to ride the wave of office gossip and intrigue, the fascination for the details (sordid or otherwise), and stories that will get more outrageous as they are passed along (think of the game of Chinese Whispers). Man, are you going to be popular for all the wrong reasons!

Human beings generally love a bit of good workplace scuttlebutt. Nothing is better (to take away the boredom of routine) than the juicy details of an illicit affair. You will need to endure preying eyes that scrutinise and judge you as you walk by and whisperings about you in the lunchroom – this will happen all day, every day while you are at work. What a vicious bunch! The Roman Senate was tame compared to today's workplace gossipmongers because the knives will be out the moment your affair becomes public knowledge. That is a whole level of hell you didn't see coming.

Not only have the waters been muddied because of this affair, but you now must deal with your emotions and turn up for work with **him** being there and the piranhas in a feeding frenzy

The Office Romance Gone Bad

five days a week. The level people will stoop to for a juicy bit of news about someone they work with is shameless.

Having an affair with a married man is like putting a gun to your head. Having an affair with a married man you work with is like loading the gun and spinning the barrel. When things go wrong between you, it's like pulling the trigger.

The result may end up with either you or him (but generally you, if you work for the guy) eventually having to leave the job and either transfer or look for something else entirely because it will become unbearable in that toxic environment. Each night you go home, your mind can't decide whether to completely shut down and sleep for 16 hours or stay awake, thinking about the horror.

Unless you are both just colleagues and can rise above the affair and compartmentalise what happened between you to the degree that you can work amicably together and carry on regardless. That is a good outcome in this scenario – rare, but good!

Oh, and it was remiss of me to mention if his wife found out because, hell, what if she works there as well? Just don't go there!

CHAPTER 31

His Loss

Throughout this book, we have focused on the loss you are experiencing if things go south and your relationship with your married man ends. But, ultimately, it will be his loss. As much as he will not admit it – not to you, himself or anybody else – your relationship had substance (even if it was only just sex), and you were part of each other's lives for a time.

If you think of all the people you have met throughout your life, from childhood to this man, you have always been left with an impression of them. No matter who it was, you will be impacted by them to some degree – whether in a positive, neutral or negative way. You pick up vibes, energy, feelings and emotions and keep memories of that person.

The experiences we share with other people are what weave the fabric of our lives. Every person we meet will impart something of themselves, and we take on the lessons they are trying to teach us, consciously or subconsciously. These lessons and the journey we share with them are part of our growth as human beings. Sometimes these lessons are hard and cruel – and the lesson will be how not to be treated – but there are times when the lesson is beautiful, and as a result we thrive and grow as a person.

When I asked you earlier to write down your feelings from this relationship, both the good and the bad, it is important to read back what you wrote with a neutral observation regarding your feelings and experience. The good aspects are just as important as the bad in the larger scheme of things, and you will notice how your feelings now may have changed.

Your married man is no different. You both were brought together – whether by chance, design, divine providence or sheer luck – to share an experience and teach you both (consciously or otherwise) what you need to learn from each other. Yes, this may sound a little left field, but if you understand this truth, you can cope better with the *why*.

If he has any integrity, he will feel your loss just as much as you will his. But that does not mean he will act on those feelings, because there will be larger issues at play that he cannot ignore or dismiss.

If nothing else, know that you gave him one of the best chapters of his life; you taught him about himself, about love and about his worth as a man. These may be attributes his wife had not given him for a long time, so even though he moved on, you were instrumental in making him feel whole again. That will be a plus to you, and even though you may think you are

His Loss

alone in your feelings, he will be feeling it too. But like I said, he may not admit it or want to come back, but you impacted him, which is a good thing on your part.

Think of your journey together as two trains travelling on separate lines. They come together and travel parallel for a time before they part and go on their own journeys, so just roll with it!

CHAPTER 32

A Word About Your Inner Voice

Everyone has **Spidey senses** – it may be that little tingling in the back of your neck. It may be your inner voice whispering to you, or even perhaps a feeling in your gut that something's not right or telling you from within to go for it; some call it *intuition*.

Not everyone listens to their gut or what they feel because they might not understand that sense or it's contrary to what they want to do (Hey, we all have free will, but not everyone is in tune with their hunches.). But this is your inner guide speaking to you – your inner compass madly spinning, alarm bells warning or alerting you. Our ears may prick up, but we do not always listen to that 'feeling'.

Is He Ever Going to Leave His Wife?

So, you get a bad feeling about something. Still, despite all the warnings going off in your head like the fireworks display on New Year's Eve, you do it anyway, only to say to yourself, 'I knew this was a mistake!' That was your intuition discharging and forewarning you, 'DON'T DO IT!'

Well, you keep seeing this guy, and even though the alarm bells have been clanging like Big Ben in your head for some time, you keep seeing him anyway. Then, when he's ripped out your heart and danced on it, you wonder why you didn't trust all that inner commotion.

There are also degrees of warnings you will receive – not only bells tinkling or cannons firing but more subtle vibes. For instance, you meet someone for the first time and, whether straight away or well into the conversation, you begin to sense something about this person. Are they on the level, or do you need to run the hell away from him as fast as you can? Again, your instincts will tell you. Listen to them!

With someone you have known for a while, however, things can be different with your intuition because that person is familiar to you, and they are your friend. What you start picking up on may be your intuition sensing something not quite right with them. This may indicate an issue they may be going through or feeling, and you may be picking up on their unhappiness or troubles. This is far different from your Spidey senses triggering when you know there is danger present.

This intuition is also the best way to tell whether someone is good to be with **and keep in your life**. It's a simple test to check how you feel after you have left that person; the encounter may

A Word About Your Inner Voice

have been pleasant and polite, but there was this uneasiness within you. Listen to that!

With some people, you feel positive and good about having been with them, and you are happy and buoyant. It was a joy to be with them even if they shared their troubles; not a negative vibe in sight. That person is good for your soul, so see more of them.

If, however, you feel, in any way, negative or down after leaving that person and want to head for the nearest medicine cabinet to grab a razor blade and end it all despite spending a reasonably good time with them, your intuition is telling you to steer clear of that sucker, big time.

Our senses and intuition are key to understanding the best path to take, whether it be what is good for you or what you stay the hell away from. Once you listen to this inner voice, guide, intuition, hunch, vibe, energy or whatever name you identify with, then it will never steer you wrong. You just have to be aware, take notice, and act on it.

Trust yourself and your Spidey senses.

CHAPTER 33

Recovery Road

How to get over your married man: Positive things you can do for yourself

Throw a celebratory wake

OK, now that you're ready to stop obsessing over this man and move forward, let's start with getting a few of your friends together and make an occasion out of this. Get a few bottles of bubbly and lots of great music you can dance to. The ones suggested in this book are a start. Let the girls know you want to get over this guy, so you are planning a wake because your relationship died!

Ditch anything that reminds you of him

Get rid of everything you have of his. You do not want reminders of him around the place to open old wounds. Pack up whatever he gave you – jewellery, lingerie, clothing, trinkets – and ditch, sell or give them to charity. Those sentimental, gushy cards – shred them. If there are any photos or text messages on your phone – delete, delete, delete! And while you are at it, unfriend or even block him on social media.

By doing this, his energy will lessen and will no longer have a hold on you. Someone I once knew was so incensed when they found out their partner was having an affair that they dragged the mattress they shared outside to the back lawn and set fire to it.

Do a cleanse

Do what it takes to eliminate his energy from your home by burning sage sticks, salting the perimeter of your home, or just giving the place a good airing and cleaning. No more reminders of him to set off your thoughts and emotions. Wash away those tears and clean away those fears (of him entering your head).

Take a class or do a course

Next, you will need to occupy your mind with something absorbing. Learn something new, join a creative group or take up a hobby – anything to keep you absorbed and limit thinking of him. Enrol in a Technical and Further Education (TAFE) class or course, take up a different sport or go to the gym (or go to a different gym if that is where you met him), go for a walk or a run. Doing this will set your feet on a different path and lead you in a new direction.

Take up yoga or meditation or some other gentle aspect to calm you, improve your physical and mental health and uplift your energy. By being focused, you concentrate your thoughts and enrich yourself and your well-being. By meeting new people, you interact with new energy and get out of the house to stop yourself from brooding.

Invest in yourself

Make yourself a priority and learn to nurture and love yourself the way you needed when you were a child. Be the parent you never had, so you can heal the little child that is now a fractured woman.

Be gentle and kind to yourself. The more you invest in your life, the more you will be able to grow as a person. You do not have to shell out money, if that is an issue; there are so many YouTube videos or information on the internet about helping you better yourself.

Write him a letter (but don't send it)

Again, writing is a powerful aid to overcome the negativity and loss you feel and sort out your thoughts. I suggest you physically write on paper because the connection of physically handwriting on paper than merely typing on a keyboard is so much more powerful – but if the keyboard works for you, then great!

In your letter, explain everything about how you allowed him to treat you. Be honest with this (e.g., I allowed you to keep seeing me despite knowing you are married. I allowed myself to live in hope.). As much as this may hurt to admit, you had a say in how the relationship progressed. If you are honest with yourself, you will take responsibility for your part in the affair so you can open that wound to the light, and from that you let go of the baggage and heal.

No blame is intended here, and this is not an exercise in punishment. You were a victim in all this, but by taking responsibility for your part in things and pointing them out in a letter, you are owning your 'miss-take' and recognising the role you played in this relationship.

This can be a confronting exercise and will bring up negative emotions and hurt, but that is a good thing. While you write your thoughts and feelings down, you are releasing that negativity from your body, and you will be able to start healing. Yay, you!

You may find yourself writing several pages, yet there is more to say. Keep on writing until you are finished, until you have extracted every emotion within you and written it on paper. Then, when you are ready, shred what you wrote, go outside and safely burn those pages and release them to the universe or hit 'Select All and Delete'!

Transform your life

You are on your way to being a clean slate, a fresh chapter and a new woman. Be proud of yourself for what you have achieved already by ridding yourself of that negative element and investing wisely in the most important person you know: You!

You have gone up a rung in the ladder, and because you will not accept any less for yourself, if it comes around again, you will be ready because you have learned that valuable lesson of self-importance, respect and are equipped to deal with it. You will be able to live the life you want on your terms, having learned and owning a truth about yourself and what you will and won't allow to happen. The way the world works is simple – whatever you believe for yourself will eventuate. (I am so excited for you!)

The best revenge is a fabulous life

This is the only revenge worth pursuing. Once you have blossomed and are the woman you were always meant to be – beautiful, successful and happy – life begins to change course to support you. So, go do all the things you dreamed of. Work at achieving those goals, and if you happen to post your successes on social media and somehow 'Numb Nuts' learns what's happened with you, this teaches him what an awesome woman you are. Good for you!

Take it easy

The secret to dealing with all this is to take one day at a time, and if that is too much to bear, take one hour or one moment

Is He Ever Going to Leave His Wife?

at a time without him. Added together, each moment you have survived becomes a series of victories for you until you've made it through another day and then another (you do this anyway every time he leaves you). You just need to change your mindset (by focusing on you) and break everything down into small, manageable moments.

---
*Take inspiration from the song
'Unstoppable' by Sia*

CHAPTER 34

Take Back Your Power, Girl!

Grapes must be crushed to make wine.

Diamonds form under pressure.

Olives are pressed to release oil.

Seeds grow in darkness.

Whenever you feel crushed, under pressure, pressed or in darkness,

You're in a powerful place of transformation.

Trust the process.

Throughout this book, I have mentioned taking back your power.[21] While you may be sceptical and think this may not apply to you, I assure you it applies to everyone. When you understand how this can change your life, see the benefits of owning your power and stop allowing others to dictate how you should live, you will become more confident and respected and begin to grow as a person.

Learn to say no.

When needed, say no and say it with the conviction of an evangelist at a pulpit! People pleasers, and most women in general, say yes to something we know we need to say no to because it is easier. We usually regret it afterwards and may even try and get out of the agreement. This comes from not wanting to hurt people, wanting to please them, wanting to be accepted and wanting to be liked. All we're doing is giving away our power to get on someone's good side.

> I use the word *Nup!* instead of *no* on less serious occasions because, although it means the same thing, it is not as harsh on me and the other person. Try it. On more serious matters, a 'Hell No!' will suffice before walking away.

Not everyone needs saving, so stop that approach.

We all want to help people and even save them, but you are giving away your power to that person by doing so. You may bust a gut for them, only to end up exactly where you started while they move on; now they are all fixed. So, stop giving away your power to those who don't want it.

How do you know they don't want it? They do not take your advice or take up your help or suggestions but are happy for you to do the heavy lifting for them.

Toxic people will sap your energy and power, so ditch them.

You are a bright shining light of goodness. You will come across those who will take everything they can from you, energy- wise and anything else: your time, your resources, your advice and knowledge and even your money. They will literally suck the life out of you like an energy vampire, so learn to stop when your Spidey senses begin to bristle and before you are exhausted from busting a gut for them.

Don't play the blame game.

It is so easy to give your power away to your past, to all the people who wronged you and left you with emotions that have festered and manifested within you. Treat the past like a book. Each chapter has been read, so let it go to where it belongs: in the past.

Your power returns to you when you forgive yourself for allowing things that you had no control over to happen to you. While you will not forget what happened, learn to forgive **yourself** and regain your power. Be the parent of that little child in you who was wronged, and treat her now the way she deserved – with kindness, sympathy and love and hugs. Lots of hugs!

Trust yourself.

There is no time better than this very second to start trusting yourself. Out of this whole world, the only person who knows you best, who is there for you, who has your back is you. You do not need to wait to do this; once you listen to your inner voice, gut or instincts and follow that line, then you regain your power big time.

Walking alone is the most powerful thing you can do for yourself.

Yes, it can be terrifying to walk alone, even if it is for a short time. There may be no one to hold your hand or have your back, but the strength you gain from relying on yourself builds exponentially. Don't be scared. You learned to walk, talk, ride a bike, drive a car and deal with stuff in your life; walking alone is just another learning experience.

If you would like to explore this further, there is an excellent book about being alone, titled Alonement: How to be Alone and Absolutely Own It by Francesca Specter.[22]

Reclaim your power.

Remember all those fun things you used to do and have not done since? Now is the time to engage in those wonderful, feel-great activities, get-togethers or what used to make you feel alive. Have fun and leave yourself with a sense of being. What made you feel great back then was 'you within your power', which is what you want to get back.

Take Back Your Power, Girl!

Your power is your lifeblood, your strength and your superpower. It is yours alone. So, do not give it away to anyone again! You go, girl. You've got this!

CHAPTER 35

To Sum Up His Excuses

The established line of 'I can't leave my wife (for whatever reason)' is based solely on his fear of the unknown or pure selfishness. He may be anxious about so many things because these issues and anxieties are very real to him. Here's a list:

The kids.

The kids are a perfect excuse for not being able to budge from his relationship. He thinks it makes him look like a caring and selfless dad, and he knows you won't really object to this.

Is He Ever Going to Leave His Wife?

Divorce will break him.

Divorce is very costly, and the likelihood of him letting go of whatever he and his missus have accumulated together? Never! Got his priorities set, that one!

There is a stigma about being divorced.

Even in today's tolerant society, as soon as a man announces he is divorced, the questions that come to mind are 'What happened? Why did she leave you? What's wrong with you?'

Not ready to bail on her.

The timing is not right for whatever reason. He may be slowly gearing up to it, but he's not ready to jump ship just yet.

Being alone is not a thing for him.

He may be fearful of being alone if he leaves his wife and things don't turn out with you. Dating again just scares him silly.

He's such a considerate guy who doesn't want to hurt anyone.

Because there are so many people in the mix to consider, hurting those he loves will hurt him too. But isn't he hurting you every time he's with you and then leaves? So, it's OK that you are the one he hurts, then?

To Sum Up His Excuses

Why rock the boat?

Hey, if no one is complaining and everyone knows their place, sticks to the script and doesn't want more than they are getting, then there's no reason to upset the apple cart.

He is so cocky, he even told you he's not leaving her.

How did that conversation go? 'I'm having a great time with you, babe, but this will not develop into anything more because I have a wife!'

There's you, there's the wife – life is good!

If he has you, and he also has his wife to go home to, what possible reason is there for him to leave her? He has **everything** he needs and wants in his life – and that isn't going to change any time soon.

Yeah, but I still have feelings for her …

He still loves his wife, but he's cheating on her. How does that work? Unless they are both in a free marriage, there is no reason for him to be with another woman. None!

CHAPTER 36

He **Will** Leave His Wife if …

the type of job he has is a factor.

Certain professions attract a high divorce rate because of the nature of the job, so those in any of the Forces head the list.

he is really unhappy.

There is 'dissatisfied' unhappy, and then there is 'miserable' unhappy. If he has reached a level of despondency with his marriage, it might not take much persuading to leave it.

she is abusing him.

Several different types of abuse – not just physical but psychological, emotional, monetary and verbal – negatively affect his mental health. (Take this cautiously until you have solid evidence this statement is true.)

he tells you he is leaving her and then tells her.

He's had enough, and there is no rational reason for him to stay with her other than convenience. So, he starts actively extricating himself from the marriage.

he begins divorce proceedings

He has engaged the services of an attorney and has started divorce proceedings.

he starts to dissolve his marriage.

He actively begins to split the union by dividing assets, home contents, property, money and anything they hold jointly.

he prefers your company and spends a lot more time with you.

Suppose his home life has deteriorated to the point where they are just two people living together but having separate lives. In that case, the marriage is over, so he spends more time with you.

he cares about you and how you feel.

He is investing emotion and care for your well-being. He genuinely wants to know you are safe, well and happy and ensures he does what he can to make these things happen.

he doesn't care who sees you together.

When he feels comfortable walking down the street, hand in hand with you, that is a sure sign that he does not care who sees you together because it no longer matters to him.

he talks to you on the phone when his wife is with him.

Unless he is living dangerously, his wife knows he is on the outer and moving on with his life. She probably is, too, so taking a call from you in front of her is not a big deal.

he talks about your future together.

His plans are not just talk to keep you hooked. Instead, he makes realistic and feasible plans that include you and asks for your opinion and contribution.

he is there for you.

Say, 10.30 at night you have a plumbing emergency. You text him to let him know what happened and that you are getting a plumber in the morning. But within no time, he is there for you, fixing the problem.

he makes plans to meet up again.

You enjoy each other's company, and before he leaves, he checks to see when he can see you again. He is fitting in with your plans and not just fitting you in.

there are no excuses, just action.

Instead of giving you excuses about why he hasn't done something he promised to do, he will tell you after it has been done. No messing about or avoiding the issue.

his priorities are with you.

Despite his family commitments, you are his priority. Yes, there will be times when he must be there for his kids in whatever capacity, but only for the kids.

you both know there is substance, not just sex.

There is completeness to your relationship. You are easy with each other, happy, and your love grows. There is fairness regarding doing your best for each other, and you are not tied to his agenda.

he is honest with you.

There are no excuses or lies because he is true to you and wants this relationship to work. You can talk to and ask him about anything, and he will tell you the truth. His body language will tell you if he is lying, and your gut feeling will start giving you signals if he is not on the level.

he takes you to meet his parents.

He told his parents about you after he told them his marriage was over and had already started dissolving that relationship. Big step this is, but there is no denying he is serious about you.

your gut feeling is a good one.

Everything about him feels good. There are no doubts about his integrity towards you, and your trust in his genuine love for you is real. No weird vibes or senses are bristling because he is the real deal.

CHAPTER 37

Breakdown as to Why He Is **NOT** Leaving His Wife

RED FLAGS in a nutshell.

Your relationship is top secret.

No one – **no one** – knows about you. Isn't that thrilling? (Maybe he's a spy – your own personal 007!)

Notice how any future plans do not include you?

He talks about stuff he has mapped out five years from now, and none of his plans includes you. Why is that? (He's probably just forgetful!)

Is He Ever Going to Leave His Wife?

His favourite subject is talking about his family.

Like a proud rooster crowing over his brood, he talks a lot about his family. (Well, if they mean that much to him, then what is he doing with you?)

He never has anything good to say about his wife.

So, how did he get tangled up with her in the first place if she was that bad? (I'll bet it's more like she is just reacting to his nonsense.)

Promises. Promises that he never keeps.

'Yes, as soon as I get home, I'll tell her it's over. I couldn't do it the last 30 times I tried because (fill in the blank!).'

He can't give you a straight answer as to why he can't leave his wife.

When you ask him the question, and he gives you a 'Dunno!', take this as a sign he is not at all serious about you or considering a future with you. (You don't know why you're not leaving your wife? Seriously? Clearly, the two neurons in your head that pass as your brain have collided too many times!)

If you weren't such a beautiful woman, he wouldn't be with you.

Breakdown as to Why He Is NOT Leaving His Wife

Don't take this as a compliment because this is all about making him look good, and you're nothing more than another string to his bow! (Use that string from said bow to tie a reef knot around his – never mind!)

Like a broken record, he's 'always so unhappy in his marriage!'

Does he complain for the sake of conversation? Does he want you to feel sorry for him, wallowing in the unhappiness his marriage brings him, like, every time he's with you? (Jeez, mate, you make the grim reaper look like a fun guy!)

Sex, sex and more sex – that's about it, really!

There is no real substance to your relationship, just a physical side. He may say that he loves you, but he is confusing being in love with you with being in lust with you. As I said, no substance! (Just say to him that you just want to talk about stuff and no sex, see how quick he starts canoodling!)

Can't be with you today because he has family stuff he can't get out of.

OK, these things happen, but if he is prioritising his wife and kids over you, then it's time to consider why he is putting you in last place. (That's 'last place' after the wife, kids, pets, motorbike, poker game, footy, Other Woman – need I go on?)

Is He Ever Going to Leave His Wife?

Divorce is always going to happen ... somewhere in the distant future.

He tells you that as soon as he gets home, he will do something about his situation and end his marriage. Except, the next time you see him, he is still married and acts like all is well with the wife, so there's no need to say anything to her. Why poke that sleeping bear? (No need to ask him how she took the news because it never happened, and he'll just say, 'What news?')

The excuses for not leaving are always valid (to him).

He can get creative with why he has not said anything to his wife about wanting out of the marriage and getting divorced. 'She'll kill me!' would be the lamest. (OK, if she doesn't finish you off, then I will!)

The emotional connection between you is just not there.

Something has happened between you, and you can't seem to put your finger on it. He is different somehow – aloof, distant, moody. If you ask him what is wrong, he just replies with 'Nothing' in that tone, which means he is working himself up to tell you whatever is wrong. (Brace yourself, this news is never good.)

Let me check my schedule and see if I can fit you in, babe!

Breakdown as to Why He Is NOT Leaving His Wife

There used to be a time he could barely leave you alone and wanted to spend as much time with you as physically possible. But time has passed, and you have fallen into a routine of sorts. Now he must check to see if he is free to see you. (Really? You're actually scheduling me in!)

Yeah, I never find it hard to get a woman.

This guy has been around the block more than once. It is clear he has had other women as mistresses before you. Hell, he might even have another woman on the side besides you. (You have got to admire his stamina!)

Between you and my other lover, I like you the best.

Oh, how sweet. He likes you the best. I bet you feel like a million bucks – in debt!

Man, this guy can't lie straight in bed. Liar, liar!

A man who lies to you doesn't respect you and certainly doesn't love you. Trusting him is like trusting one of those pesky phone scammers. DON'T!

He acts, thinks and talks like he's married.

Sometimes he forgets himself. You listen to him gushing about something connected to his family. While you are happy it is going so well, he is doing your head in because everything is going so well.

He talks about the future with his family.

He's planning to fly his family somewhere fun and tropical, then they are planning that big adventure his wife has always wanted to undertake as a family – hang on, where do you fit into all this scheming?

Your relationship has progressed to this point and no further.

So, the phone rings, and it's him. 'Hey babe, how about I pop around in half an hour and get you lit?'

You sigh and, for a split second, think, *Do I want to shave my legs this week because he has a free five minutes?* 'Sorry, sweet, I'm cataloguing my receipts!'

Now he cancels on you often and at the last minute.

Yeah, work meeting.

He's pretty much a closed book and is reluctant to open up to you.

Very careful with this one. He plays his cards close to his chest, and you are always left wondering if everything is all right. Trying to get him to talk about his feelings is like prying information out of an ASIO agent.

He always talks about himself and his situation but doesn't care how you feel.

NARCISSIST WARNING!

You are his dumping-off partner – offloads his emotions and then leaves.

You: Hey Hun, I've decided to charge you by the hour, so that will be $300.00. Thanks.

Him: What? What for?

You: That's the going rate for counsellors these days. Pay up or shut up!

Losing you is not that concerning for him.

Whether well into the relationship or you're beginning to ask those tough questions about when he is leaving his wife, the time will come when you are replaced by a newer model, another Other Woman. You are dispensable, and he will not hesitate to move on to someone else. (Please insert any choice word you can think of that describes the crud!)

To Sum Up

I hope you enjoyed reading this book and, more importantly, it has helped you with some of the problems you face being involved with a married man.

As much as the evidence weighs heavily on him not leaving his wife and family, the aim of this book is not to pass judgement or tell you what to do. Instead, it is to give you informed choices to better understand the *why* of things and then help you decide what is best for you.

I had extensively researched this lifestyle choice, and the women I spoke to were invaluable for sharing their stories and truth with me. I was compelled to share what I had learned, hoping you would not suffer the same heartbreak but become a stronger and more powerful version of yourself in the process.

Whatever you decide, I wish you well. May you have a beautiful life and know how special and worthwhile you are. Remember, when one chapter ends, another one begins. So, go live your dreams, write new chapters and be happy. You deserve it!

Martess Dowling

Endnotes

1. K Soriano, 'Tell Me All I Need to Know About Narcissistic Personality Disorder', Psycom, 2022, https://www.psycom.net/personality-disorders/narcissistic.

2. C Lamothe, 'Love Bombing: 10 Signs of Over-the-Top-Love', Healthline, 2019, https://www.healthline.com/health/love-bombing.

3. Narcissistic Personality Disorder, Mayo Clinic, 2022, https://www.mayoclinic.org/diseases-conditions/narcissistic-personality-disorder/symptoms-causes/syc-20366662.

4. M Beauchamp, 'What is Breadcrumbing? A Relationship Expert Explains', Brides.com, https://www.brides.com/what-is-breadcrumbing-5105353.

5. M Beauchamp, 'What Is Gaslighting in a Relationship?', Brides.com, 2022, https://www.brides.com/gaslighting-in-relationships.

6. P Brian, '15 signs he's not as nice as you think (and you need to get away from him FAST)', Hack Spirit, 2022, https://hackspirit.com/signs-he-is-not-a-nice-guy/.

7. C Grainger, 'Stonewalling: What It Is and How to Cope', Brides.com, 2022, https://www.brides.com/stonewalling-in-relationships-5268220.

8. C Meyer, 'How to Recognize Signs of Passive-Aggressive Behavior in Your Spouse', Brides.com, 2022, https://www.brides.com/passive-aggressive-behaviors-in-marriage-1102423.

9. H Pevzner, 'Signs You're Married to a Narcissist – And What to Do About It', Psycom, 2022, https://www.psycom.net/narcissist-signs-married-to-a-narcissist.

10. A Altınok & N Kılıç, 'Exploring the associations between narcissism, intentions towards infidelity, and relationship satisfaction: Attachment Styles as a moderator', PLOS ONE, 2020, https://journals.plos.org/plosone/article?id=10.1371%2Fjournal.pone.0242277.

11. H Mendelsohn, '10 Signs of An Emotionally-Abusive Relationship', Brides.com, 2022, https://www.brides.com/signs-of-an-emotionally-abusive-relationship-5112027.

12. S Ciminelli, 'The Five Stages of Grief – A Journey', Australian Institute of Family Counselling, 2018, https://www.aifc.com.au/five-stages-of-grief-journey/.

13. 'The 5 Stages of Grief and Self-Care', Bethel Funerals, 2019, https://www.bethelfunerals.com.au/5-stages-of-grief-self-care/.

14. Visit Beyond Blue at https://www.beyondblue.org.au.

15. A Doughty, 3 Secrets to Letting Go, video file, YouTube, 2022, https://www.youtube.com/watch?v=8RVamUBXAIc.

16. J Bowlby & M Ainsworth, The Origins of Attachment Theory, 1992, p 28, ch 24, https://www.simplypsychology.org/attachment.html.

17. Oxford Dictionary, s.v. 'mistress', https://www.oxfordlearnersdictionaries.com/us/definition/american_english/mistress.

18. T Miller, There are only 3 kinds of homewreckers in the world, YourTango, New York, 2022, https://www.yourtango.com/self/types-homewreckers-world.

19. J Bauer, His Secret Obsession: How to Get Inside the Mind of Any Man, Lulu.com, 2022, https://beirresistible.com/his-secret-obsession/?campaignid=167384166&adgroupid=40440391658&feeditemid=&targetid=kwd-342216335266&loc_interest_ms=&loc_physical_ms=9070964&matchtype=e&network=g&device=c&devicemodel=&creative=330346293995&keyword=james%20bauer%20his%20secret%20obsession&placement=&target=&adposition=&gclid=Cj0KCQiAqOucBhDrARIsAPCQL1YFEwZ7AVeaEycttqZCThnV_jqVqW3JWTg67FTH11S455YyVp5c6VsaArjlEALw_wcB.

20. A Pease, Body Language: How to Read Others' Thoughts by Their Gestures, Sheldon Press, 1997.

21. L Saviuc, '7 Powerful Steps to Take Back Your Power and Be True to Yourself Again', Purpose Fairy, 2021, https://www.purposefairy.com/86961/take-back-your-power/.

22. F Specter, Alonement: How to be Alone and Absolutely Own It, Quercus Publishing, 2022, https://www.alonement.com/book.

Acknowledgements

I would like to thank my dear, darling husband, Alan, for believing in me and always fully supporting everything I do, for being the love of my life, my best friend and teacher.

To our beautiful son, Tim, our little miracle whom we love with all our hearts and are so proud of, especially for always being such an inspiration to me – you are my hero.

My dear Dad, who is such a good friend and mentor, and Mum in heaven, whom I miss. I hope I have made you both proud.

To Anne and Mary for being such a wonderful family.

The dearest and most genuine 'earth-bound angels' I have the privilege of calling my long-time friends – Barbara, Colleen, Diana, Gail, Josie, Kelly, Lindsey, Michele, Sandy, Sharon and Trudy. You have all saved me in many ways, along with their equally wonderful families for being there when times were tough.

Is He Ever Going to Leave His Wife?

To these fabulous individuals who shared my journey and taught me so much about how to find myself – Bernadette, Carmel, Cathy, Elisabeth, Helen, Jackie, Kate, Marie, Maritza, Martina, Martin and Vera. My grateful thanks. You have all been instrumental in shaping the person I have become.

And finally, with gratitude to these beautiful souls who were my teachers and each changed the course of my life – Alan, Tim, Jeremy, Janet, Juan, Laura, Marnie, Ross. With all my heart, thank you.

About the Author

Born in Malta in 1961, and two years later immigrated to Australia to the seaside suburb of Glenelg with her parents, this is where she loved to watch the activity along the beach and developed a fascination with people. Throughout her early school life, she loved to draw, be creative and organise school plays. She became involved in the school newspaper in high school, and encouraged by Mrs Jerome, her love of writing grew.

Meeting and marrying her beloved husband, Alan, they spent nine years in the mining town of Broken Hill, New South Wales, where her creative flair came to the fore. She established a cake-decorating business, culminating in her taking out awards in three states – New South Wales, Victoria and South Australia – then took out a national title before having her prize-winning cake featured in the Australian Women's Weekly.

Martess had a beautiful baby boy after she and Alan moved to Adelaide. When he began school, she worked in retail, on a tarot line, sewing wedding dresses, then became a marriage celebrant and loved every second. She still writes and lives a

Is He Ever Going to Leave His Wife?

spiritual life with her husband in their beach suburb home with their beloved cats, Dalia Grace and Pip Saru.

Notes

www.ingramcontent.com/pod-product-compliance
Lightning Source LLC
Chambersburg PA
CBHW050349120526
44590CB00015B/1620